I0418924

Published by Louisiana State University School of Art & Louisiana State University Museum of Art
Distributed by Louisiana State University Press
Copyright ©2013 Louisiana State University School of Art & Louisiana State University Museum of Art
All rights reserved

Louisiana State University Museum of Art
Shaw Center for the Arts, 5th Floor
100 Lafayette Street
Baton Rouge, LA 70801
www.lsumoa.com

Louisiana State University School of Art
Glassell Gallery, Shaw Center for the Arts
100 Lafayette Street
Baton Rouge, LA 70801
www.glassellgallery.org • www.art.lsu.edu

Louisiana State University Union Art Gallery
216 LSU Student Union
Box 25123
Baton Rouge, LA 70803
www.lsu.edu/union

ISBN: 978-0-8071-5321-5

This book is published by Louisiana State University School of Art and Louisiana State Museum of Art in conjunction with the exhibition
Peter Shire: One Retrospective, Three Venues, January 31– April 14, 2013 at Louisiana State University School of Art Glassell Gallery,
Louisiana State University Museum of Art and the Louisiana State University Union Art Gallery in Baton Rouge, Louisiana.

Artwork by Peter Shire
Curated by Natalie Mault, Malia Krolak, Judith Stahl

Design and Production:

Producer: Kitty Pheney
Faculty Advisors: Lynne Baggett, Rod Parker
Creative Director: Jeremy Grassman
Designer: Luisa Fernanda Restrepo Pérez
LSU School of Art: Graphic Design Student Office

Photography: Joshua White/JWPictures.com
Memphis Milano, S.R.L.

Printing: IPC Printing, Baton Rouge, LA

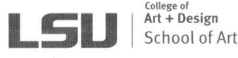
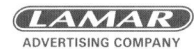

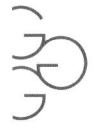
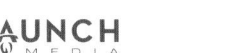
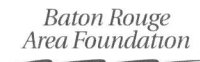
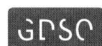
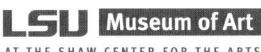

L.A. to L.A.
PETERSHIRE

at LSU, January 31 – April 14, 2013

Texts by Darius A. Spieth & Jo Lauria

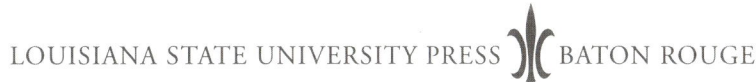

LOUISIANA STATE UNIVERSITY PRESS · BATON ROUGE

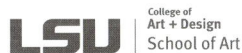 LSU | College of Art + Design | School of Art

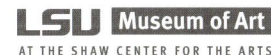 LSU | Museum of Art | AT THE SHAW CENTER FOR THE ARTS

INTRODUCTION

As we approach the centenary of the founding of the Bauhaus in 1919, the end of history seems not to have happened. Modernism and Postmodernism have come and gone, and now even the 1980s are beginning to seem almost like a golden age—a time before we were all "connected," a time before the continuous news cycle, and a time when ideas of globalization existed as much in the realm of the avant-garde, as that of the global corporate product supply chain.

The Memphis group, of which Peter Shire was a member, flourished during that era before personal computers and smartphones and expressed themselves, as Darius Spieth notes in his accompanying essay, in ways that were innovative, forceful, and optimistic. It is the sunny optimism and rejuvenating freedom of artists such as Peter Shire, who came of age in the late 1960s, merged with his subsequent disciplined, daily studio practice over the course of almost forty years that Jo Lauria refers to in her timeline of his career, which speaks volumes to today's students.

Peter Shire's work encompasses many of the disciplines we teach in the School of Art at Louisiana State University, and addresses fine art, craft, and design in the "groundbreaking nexus" identified by Jordana Pomeroy in her Foreword. In addition to the work itself, the issues it raises of the relationship between design and function, theory and practice, the past and the future are at the heart of the daily interactions between faculty, curators and students in our studios, classrooms and galleries.

A visionary seriousness of purpose combined with a lightness of touch emerges from Peter Shire's work, which is fundamentally generous, pluralistic, and inclusive. And it is this point of view that comes into exquisite alignment with our mission, values, and goals at Louisiana State University as the School of Art, The Museum of Art, and the Union Art Gallery invite the communities that sustain us to join us through exhibitions, catalog, classes, and lectures which comprehensively examine the career of this significant artist.

The efforts to shape this project have benefitted from many capable minds and hands within the School of Art, and would not have been possible without them. The School thanks Darius Spieth, Kitty Pheney, Jeremy Grassman, Luisa Restrepo Perez, the Graphic Design Student Office, Malia Krolak, and Meg Holford. The faculty Visting Artist Committee and our graduate students in the front and back offices of the School's galleries have contributed energetically, as have Chanta Franklin and Catherine Wells in the School of Art office.

The Nadine Carter Russell Chair endowment made possible Peter Shire's lecture and teaching residency in the Department of Interior Design. We appreciate the efforts of the College of Art & Design's Interim Dean, Kenneth Carpenter, Associate Dean Tom Sofranko, Development Officer Michael Robinson, as well as the college's support staff. We also extend our gratitude for the support that the Baton Rouge Area Foundation has provided through the LSU School of Art Auto Hotel Fund and the Paula Garvey Manship Fund—both of which benefit from the advice of Nadine Carter Russell.

The School of Art's exhibition and reception were made possible by the leaders, supporters, and members of the Glassell Gallery Group, as well as the many donors to the School of Art's Leadership and Gallery Support Funds at the LSU Foundation. We particularly wish to acknowledge Nadine Carter Russell, Susie Blyskal, Virginia Pearson, Renee Daigle, John and Frances Hu, Winifred Reilly, Harry Sachse for his donation to the Janice R. Sachse Visiting Artist Series, and Alfred C. Glassell, Jr. for the endowments that bear his name and which support the operations of the Glassell Gallery.

Rod Parker
Director, LSU School of Art

FOREWORD

The phrase "practically absurd" suggests more than a clever play on words when used to describe the design of Los Angeles artist Peter Shire. Shire's work poses questions that have floated about for at least a century and a half: what is the relationship between design and function, and how closely do they have to interact? *Practically Absurd: Art & Design by Peter Shire* at the LSU Museum of Art features ceramic teapots, silver, and furniture that Shire created from the 1980s to 2009, all of which have been produced as unique pieces or in limited editions.

Shire's work evokes historical dialogues about form versus function, while simultaneously heralding a world of affordable, unconventional household products popularized by Terence Conran and others. In a museum setting, the brightly colored, architectonic forms that Shire has assembled into objects for the home recall Russian Constructivists such as Kasimir Malevich. In a living room, Shire's work provides cause to ponder, "How do I work this?" to quote from the Talking Heads' 1981 single *Once in a Lifetime.* A teapot is not just a teapot when it becomes an aesthetic object that challenges its core function as a vessel for hot water.

The relationship between ornament and utilitarian objects weighed heavily on the minds of nineteenth-century British critics, who noted a growing rift between form and function. "Design," noted the artist Richard Redgrave, "has reference to the construction of any work both for use and beauty, and therefore includes its ornamentation also. Ornament is merely the decoration of a thing constructed. Ornament is thus necessarily limited, for, so defined, it cannot be other than secondary, and must not usurp a principal place."[1] Victorian design eventually ceded its place to sleek functionalism that used new technology and forms invented for twentieth-century industrial machinery. Los Angeles in the 1970s was a world where artists, designers, architects, and musicians had a sense of permission, an open arena that welcomed creative expression. Shire cites two major influences that determined the trajectory of his own work: a 1920s teapot by Marianne Brandt in an exhibition at the Pasadena Art Museum of Bauhaus design, and wood scraps at his father's carpentry work sites — the former, a precious object that firmly sent ornament into exile; the latter, modest discards of a craftsman. The fluidity of ceramics allowed Shire to establish a groundbreaking nexus among fine art, craft, and industrial design and carry it over into other areas, including furniture and silver productions.

An exhibition of Shire's remarkable oeuvre has been overdue. This first partnership between LSU's School of Art and the LSU Museum of Art has enabled the university's rich artistic resources to pool their scholarship, skills, and imagination in order to present a fresh look at Peter Shire. It is the museum's good fortune that LSU's Department of Interior Design invited Shire to serve as the Nadine Carter Russell Endowed Chair for 2013, presenting the opportunity for us to exhibit some of Shire's most seminal work. Associate Professor of Art History Darius Spieth and independent curator Jo Lauria provide a context in which to appreciate Shire's contribution to the world of art and design. Financial support from Nadine Carter Russell and underwriting from Lamar Advertising allowed us to create this catalog, which serves as the legacy for the exhibitions at the museum, the LSU Union Art Gallery, and the LSU School of Art Glassell Gallery. The exhibition would not have been possible at the museum without thoughtful loans and coordination from Donna Shire and Peter Shire. Generous contributions from Launch Media and WHLC Architecture + Schwartz/Silver enabled the museum to bring these loans to Baton Rouge. Finally, I extend my gratitude to our curator, Natalie Mault; research assistant, Lauren Barnett, and the rest of the museum's team for their organization of this project at the LSU Museum of Art.

Dr. Jordana Pomeroy
Executive Director, LSU Museum of Art

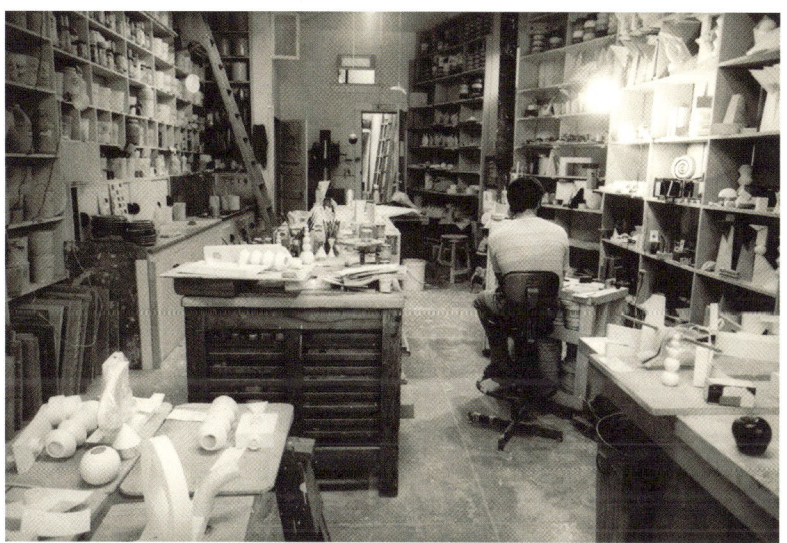

---

1   Richard Redgrave, "Supplementary Report on Design," *Exhibition of the Works of Industry of All Nations,* 1851 (London, 1852), 708.

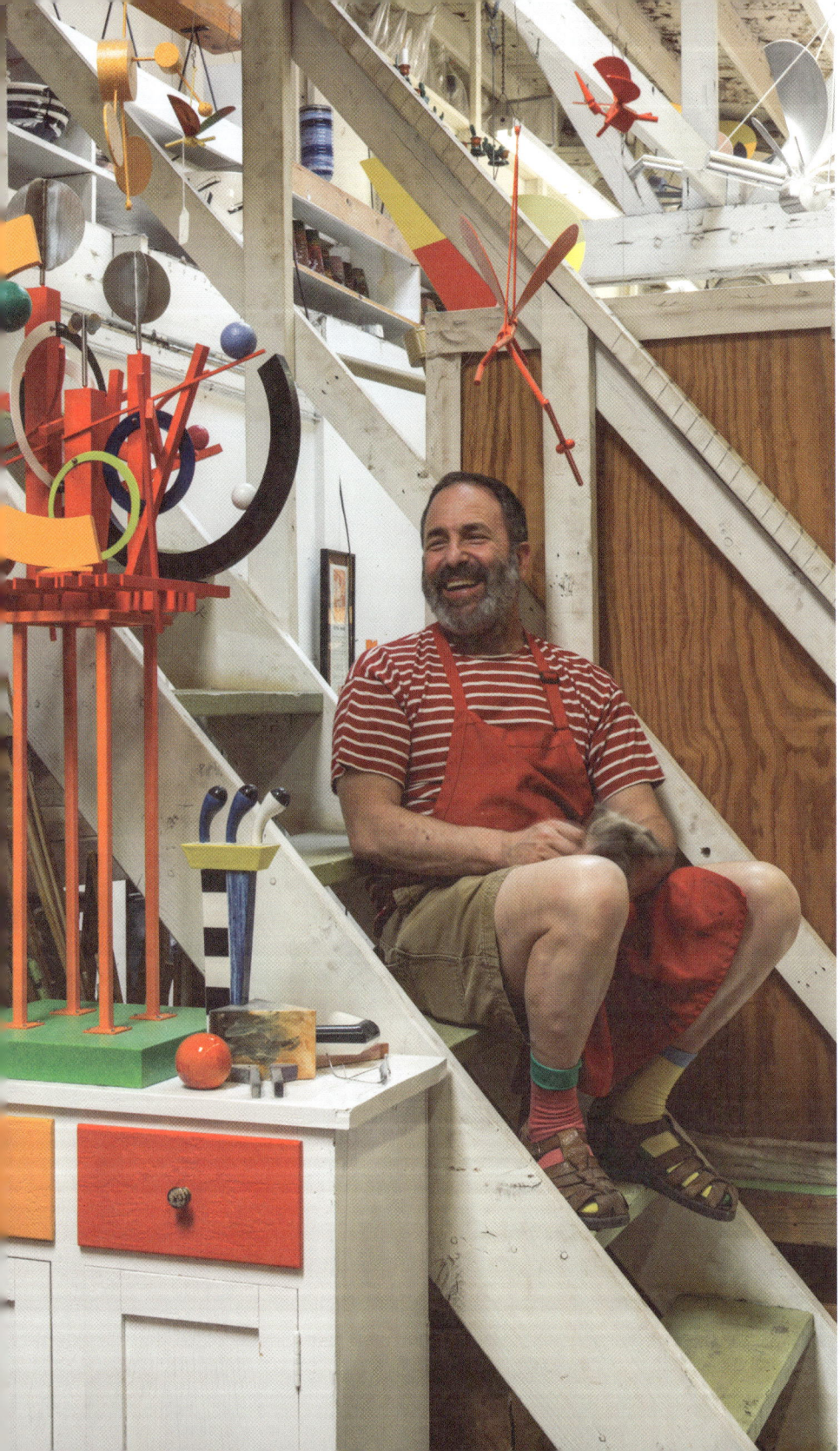

FLASH-POINTS
IN THE LIFE AND CAREER
OF ARTIST PETER SHIRE

By Jo Lauria

2012 Peter Shire in his Echo Park studio

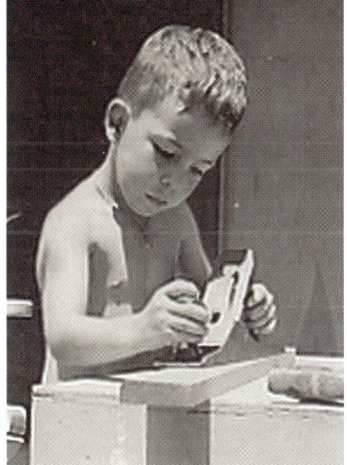

1951 Peter Shire

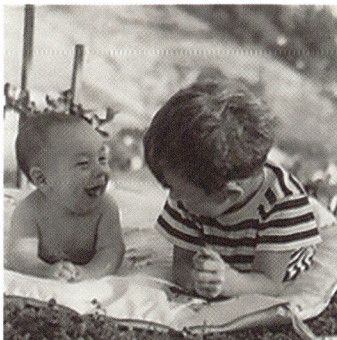

1951 Billy and Peter Shire

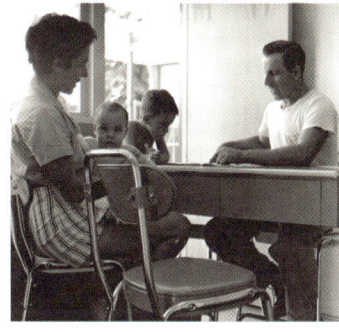

1951 The Shire Family

1947-1958

The Beginning and Early Years

Peter was born in 1947 to parents Hank and Barbara Shire. The family lived in Echo Park, California, in a home that Hank had designed and built , "with his own hands," as Peter likes to emphasize. Hank was an accomplished artist who had graduated as an illustrator from Pratt Institute (Brooklyn). However, Hank became a master carpenter as a way to support his family, which soon grew to include two sons with the arrival of Billy, Peter's younger brother, in 1951. The Shires were a very close-knit family and became tightly woven into the fabric of the Bohemian community in which they lived. In fact, Peter would establish his professional Echo Park Artist Studio in the same neighborhood where he grew up. From his father, Peter learned the values associated with making things by hand, and was encouraged from a very young age to build and tinker. Peter is quite certain there was a "transference" involved from father to son; however one wants to explain it, Peter ended up collecting hammers—it's a formidable collection in its size and variety; and Hank was given the opportunity to skillfully guide a pen, as he did his hammer, and design and illustrate several fliers and posters for Peter's studio.

Peter's hobbies as a young boy were mostly art-related. He recalls many happy Saturdays when his mother would take him to the children's art classes at the Pasadena Art Museum, or the weekend art and ceramic classes offered at the Chouinard Art Institute. Peter's first "formal" instruction in ceramics was through an art class in junior high, and he furthered his handcrafting skills as the shop foreman in a class on "Handicrafts" a few years later at Belmont High School, Los Angeles.

1959-1978

Young Adult Years, Chouinard Art Institute, Early Ceramics of the 1970s and early 1980s

Peter's destiny to become a ceramic artist was sealed when he enrolled in Chouinard Art Institute, Los Angeles in 1966 after graduating Belmont High School. Heading the ceramics program was Ralph Bacerra, and

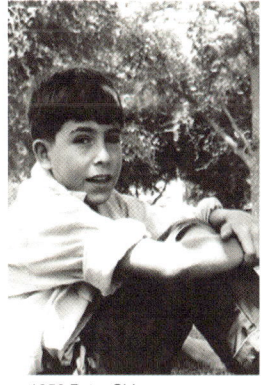

1958 Peter Shire

according to Peter, Bacerra's objective was to teach the students all the fundamentals that a classically trained potter should learn, including throwing on the potters wheel, glaze calculation, and firing kilns. Additionally, Bacerra felt it was essential for students to learn how to aesthetically display and successfully market their work, so each year the students prepared for and staged a sale of their ceramics. These Chouinard sales became highly anticipated annual events. Peter recalls: "They created a buzz around town, and were a way for many of my teapots to find happy homes." Peter graduated Chouinard with a BFA. In 1970.

Peter's work at Chouinard and during the early 1970s went through a litany of forms, experimenting with traditional pottery shapes: bowls, cups, saucers, plates, vases, teapots, and covered containers. All shapes were formed on the potters wheel or hand-built, and all attachments and extensions coaxed into place through handcrafting. From the beginning, witty humor and playfulness appeared in Peter's pots, like the drawing of a child-like sailboat adrift on the surface of "Petite Boat" teapot (1969), and the trio of colorful "Covered Jars" (1973) that looked more like spinning tops than containers made of clay. Referring to Peter's time at Chouinard, classmate Constance Saxe—who is the wife of Adrian Saxe, renowned ceramic artist—makes this assessment:

> **Peter found a voice that uses humor, is bold and sly. It is very much about his personal interests, motorcycles and cars.**

—Quoted from the publication, *Frank Lloyd, Peter Shire: Chairs*, Santa Monica: Frank Lloyd Gallery, 2007.

Peter's early ceramic pieces pointed to what would become his preference for a low-fire clay and glaze palette—a combination which allowed for the production of surfaces that could be highly controlled and manipulated. A clay teapot and pair of cups could be made to look like an elegant 1920s/30s Art Deco silver tea set in Peter's deft hands—note "Teapot and Cups-Chrome" (1973). Or a pot could sport a painterly air-brushed surface: on "Fortune Cookie Teapot" (1974), Peter applies the glaze through the commercial technique of using an air brush gun to achieve the "fade" from one glaze layer to the next. The air brush "look" was very popular

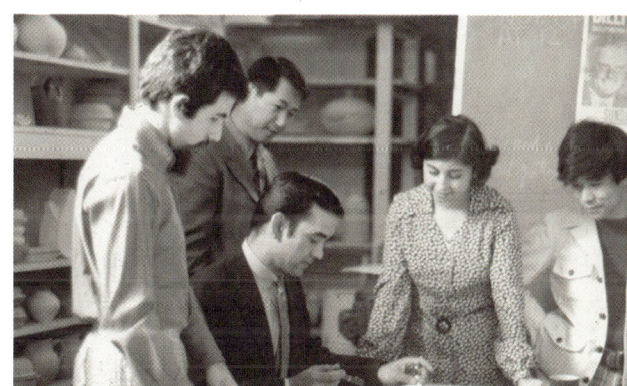

1968 Peter, Ralph Bacerra (sitting), George Gee, Juanita Jimenez, Mineo Mizuno (from left to right) Photo by Devaney Murata

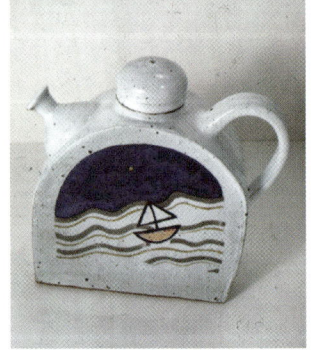

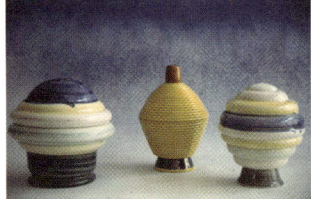

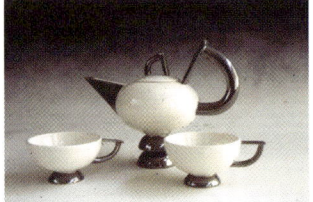

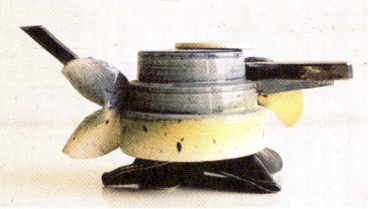

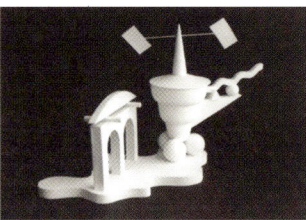

1969 Petite Boat Teapot   1973 Covered Jars   1973 Teapot & Cups-Chrome   1974 Fortune Cookie Teapot   1983 Weathervane

among illustrators, custom car finishers, and textile designers of the time. Also, the commercialization of low-fire glazes in the late 1960s early 1970s meant that every potter could pour out of the jar such high-key colors as hot-rod reds, screaming yellows, lime greens, and Malibu blues. These saturated glaze colors enabled Peter to take his palette cues from the sunny Southern California bright skies, the often garishly painted stucco homes of his neighborhood, and the neon signs of the city's night lights. He could then apply these colors at will to his expressive, highly personal pieces. It should be noted that this is a turning point. Peter explains:

" I'm only vaguely concerned about function. Forms can be referentially functional. "

1972

Peter establishes his first Echo Park Artist Studio at 1930 Echo Park Avenue where he will remain through 1997

1979

Peter and Donna Okeya are married

In the early '80s, Peter's teapots began to use color strategically to define form, and forms are based on the clarity of geometric shapes. During this period Peter becomes intrigued with the principles of the Bauhaus after viewing a Bauhaus exhibition at the Pasadena Art Museum in 1968-69. On view were works of the metal studios of the Bauhaus artists. A tea essence pot produced in 1924 by Marian Brandt specifically caught Peter's eye. Brandt was known for her sophisticated designs using the simple shapes of circle, square, and triangle. This direction—of using the reductive directness of geometric shapes—inspired Peter to make teapots such as "Hourglass" (1984) based on two stacking cones and an arc for a handle. Stacks of teapots in the Hourglass, Accordion, and Mexican Bauhaus series fill the studio shelves.

1980-1988

Peter Designs for Memphis, and the Spirit of Post Modernism in Peter's Work

In the February/March issue of *WET Magazine* 1977 (Issue 5), an article titled "TEA" was published that featured several of Peter's fanciful ceramic teapots. This issue made its way into the hands of Ettore Sottsass, one of Italy's leading designers. Ettore asked his colleague, fellow designer and journalist Matteo Thun, to journey to Los Angeles and interview Peter Shire for Italian Casa Vogue.

Matteo's journalistic jaunt would result in the publication of a two page profile on Peter, including glossy close-ups of his teapots, in Casa Vogue in May 1980. But Ettore had already established a personal relationship with Peter as he had invited Peter in the Fall of 1979 to visit Milan and meet with the Italian group of architects

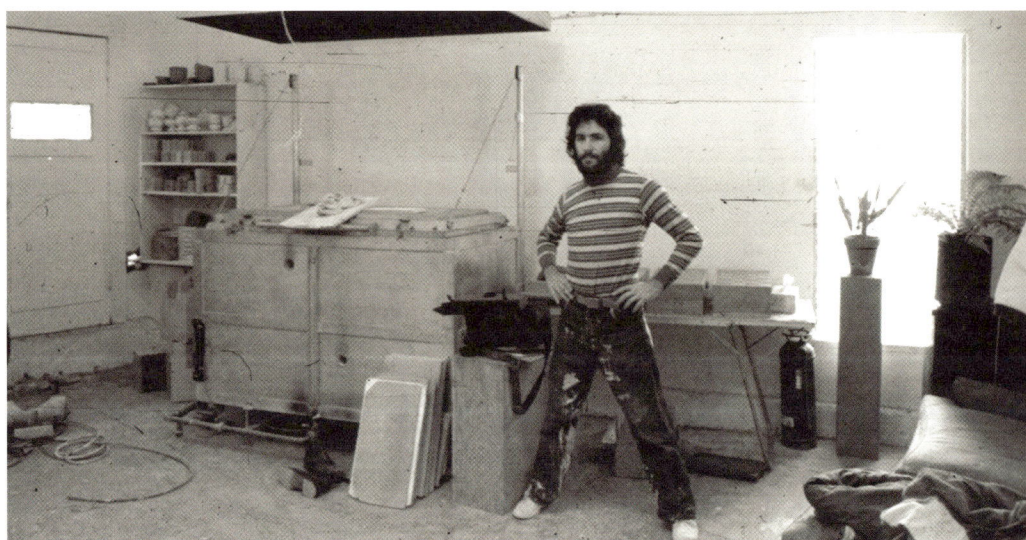

1981 Peter Shire at 1930 Echo Park Avenue

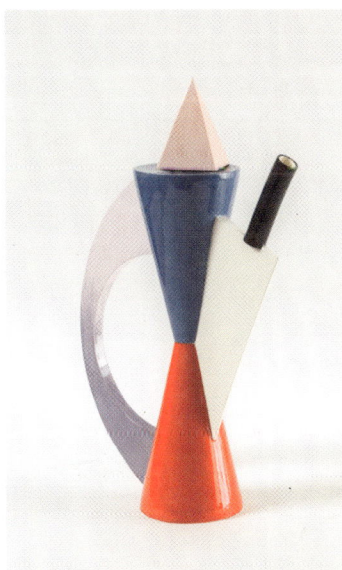

1984 Hourglass

and designers who had assembled with Ettore for the purpose of discussing a brave new world of radical design. These cutting-edge designers, who decided to call their group MEMPHIS after the Bob Dylan song— *Stuck inside of Mobile with the Memphis blues again*—vowed to make an assault on the "banality of good taste" that had been strangling the life out of contemporary design.

After Peter's visit with Ettore Sottsass and Alessandro Mendiniat Studio Alchimia in Milan in 1979, he begins an on-going collab-oration with Memphis (1980), contrib-uting designs in metalwork, sculpture, and furniture to the annual collections through 1988. Perhaps the most iconic "Shire-Memphis-design" is the Bel Air, Chair (1981) which graces the cover of the book, MEMPHIS, written by the co-founder of the design movement, Barbara Radice. The chair is a celebration of Malibu and the beach ball, the fun of the cabaret, and the amusement of acrobatics; it's a riot of colors, and a conglomeration of surprising shapes that only work together because the bolster counter-balances the ball. It's nearly impossible to look at the Bel Air, Chair without cracking a smile. Yet, despite all the visual fun, the chair is unquestionably functional its deep and substantial upholstery assure a comfortable sit.

Not true of its second generation, the Belle Aire, Chair (2010). In this iteration, Peter deconstructs the original elements of the design, and he "decides to have some fun with it, so it's a chair, only referentially. Now it's been redefined as a non-functional object." Sitting on this chair might prove a challenge, as the chair is constructed of steel and the ball protrudes into the seating space. But it has all the dimensional qualities of an engaging sculpture: simple geometric shapes defined by contrasting colors kept in tension by balanced asymmetry.

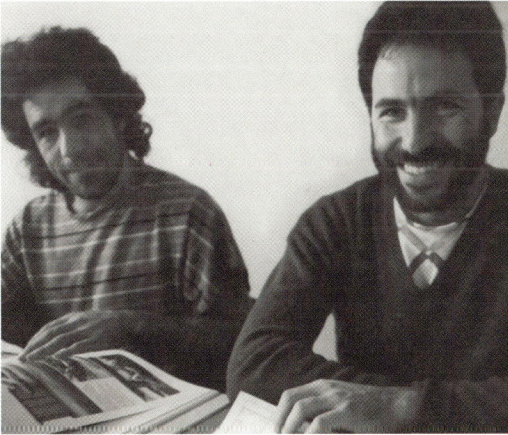

1979 Peter and Billy Shire, Studio Alchimia

1985

Peter and Ettore Sottsass attend a Glass Art Society Conference, New Orleans

During the conference, Peter and Ettore step outside of the New Orleans Art Center, where the conference was being held, for a breath of fresh air. During an impromptu moment, Ettore finds an old light bulb and decides to stage a ceremonial "passing of the idea" to Peter. A friend, who was fortuitously in tow, took the photographs of this momentous exchange from mentor to protege.

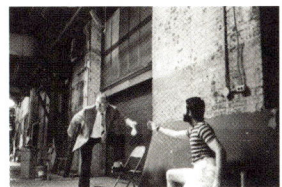 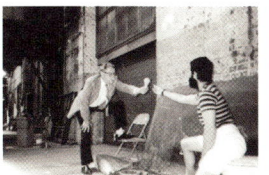 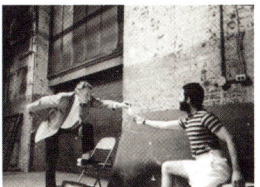

1985 Peter and Ettore, sequence shots,

Peter works everyday in his studio and constantly invents new forms

Leaving behind ceramics in the mid-80s, studio production now explodes with teapots fabricated in steel. These vanguard forms, some referred to as teapot torsos, become known for broken geometric volumes, off-kilter stances, and visible nuts and bolts. Surfaces are splashed with exuberant colors on key areas, and some give the appearance of absurd collages of mismatched components. As Peter describes them:

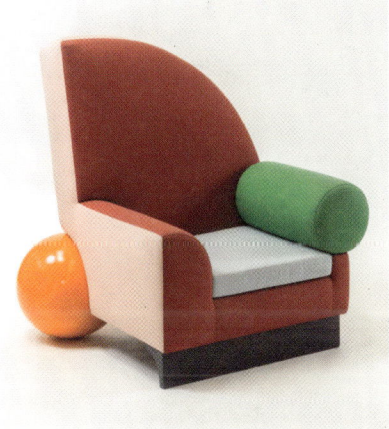

1981 Bel Air, Chair

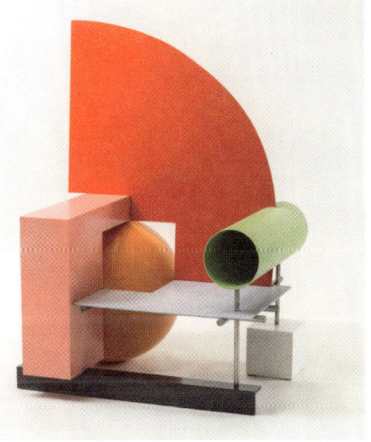

2012 Belle Aire, Chair

> **These teapots of steel contain motorcycles, bicycles, moveable lead type and the impossibility of tea. Moveable type whose system of interlocking ornaments can be composed according to their shapes, fit, yet seem to float on the page. Metal that is connected off stage. These things help comprise the composition, emotion, nostalgia and absurdity in these teapots of steel.**

—[Quoted from the publication *Gary Wong, Peter Shire, Teapots of Steel*, Chouinard Gallery: South Pasadena, 2005

The influence of Alexander Calder's "The Circus" can be seen most directly in this work. Peter had seen the film on Calder's circus many times and the film further fueled Peter's love of miniatures and his longing to recreate the excitement of going to the big-top as a kid. The "Unicyclist" installation is full of whimsy and nostalgia, and it harks back to Peter's boyhood days of building with erector sets. It also realizes his evolution of learning about trusses, suspensions, weights, balances, and counterbalances, necessary skills that have become part of his art and design practice.

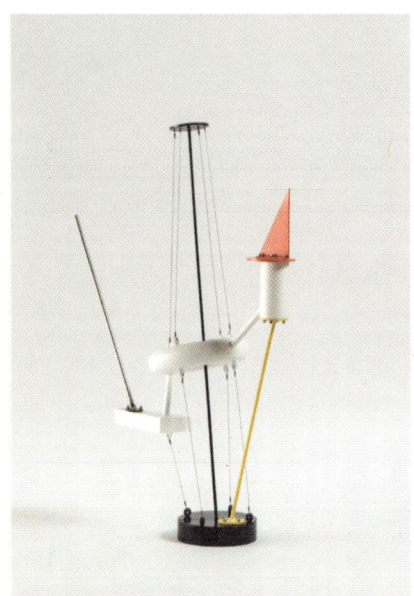
c. 1990 Micro Malevich Station

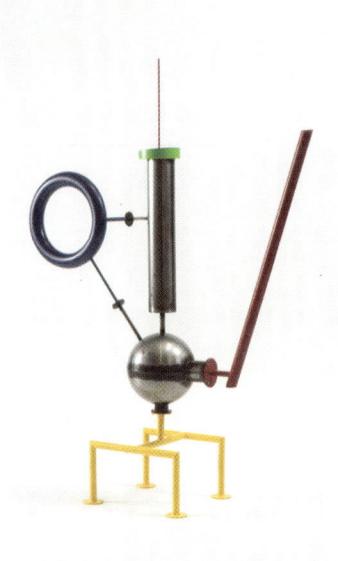
c. 1990 Giant Torso

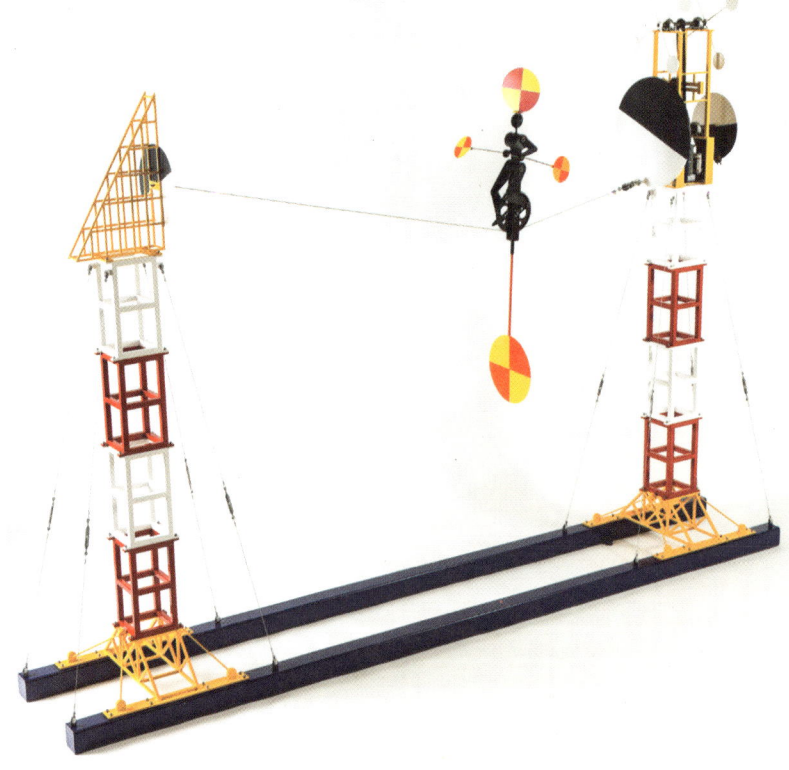
1998 Unicyclist Installation

1997
Peter moves to his new studio building, a larger facility at 1850 Echo Park Avenue, just store fronts away from his previous address

1998
Installation for Metro Station at Wilshire and Vermont Boulevards, Los Angeles

2008-2012
Peter is commissioned to do an outdoor installation for the City of West Hollywood, California

Six colorful steel sculptures—looking like abstract constructivist mobiles—are positioned amid the grass and palm trees on the median strip of Santa Monica Boulevard, West Hollywood, as a temporary installation. These graphic constructions parade along the boulevard, boldly announcing Peter's playful whimsical sensibility on a grand scale. The installation is so popular with the people of West Hollywood that it is extended for several months.

" I am a maker of things, a hand-skills guy... there is no separation between art and craft. They are all one, and a daily living experience is worthy of aesthetic consideration. "

Peter is quoted in the *Los Angeles Times* in 2007.

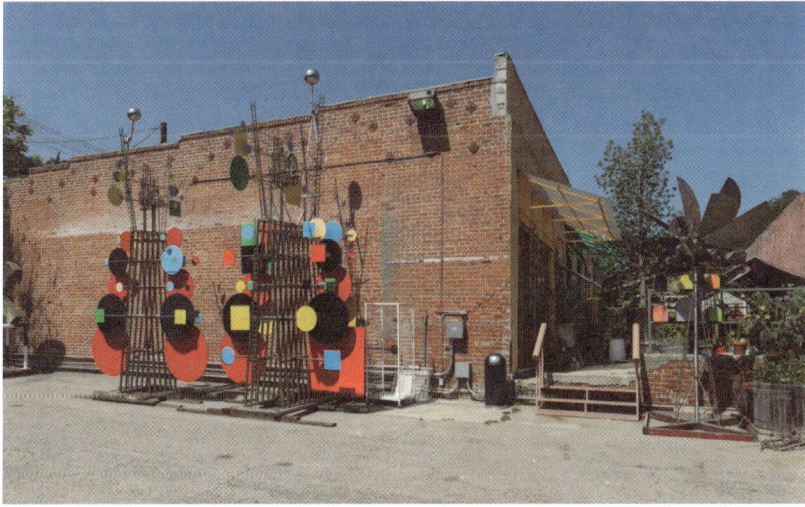

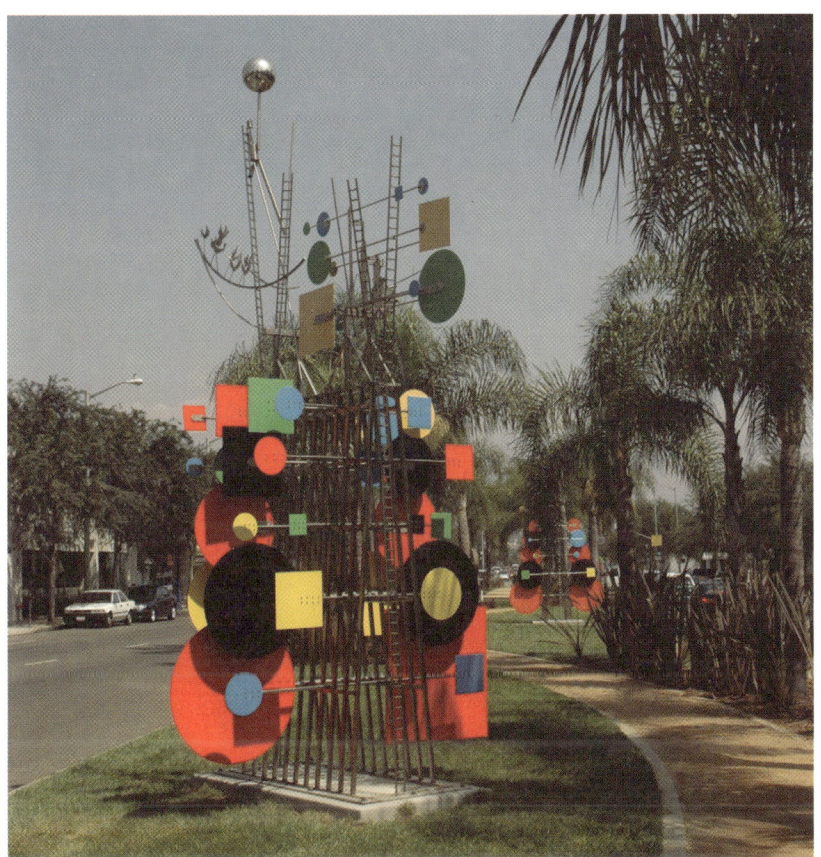

2008 Installation, City of West Hollywood, CA

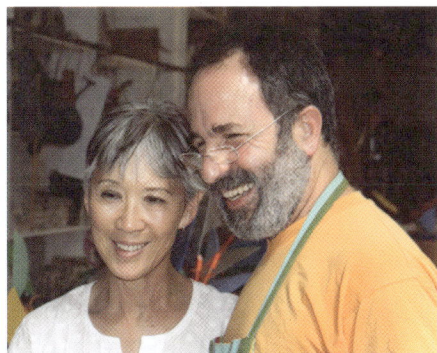

2010 Peter and Donna Shire

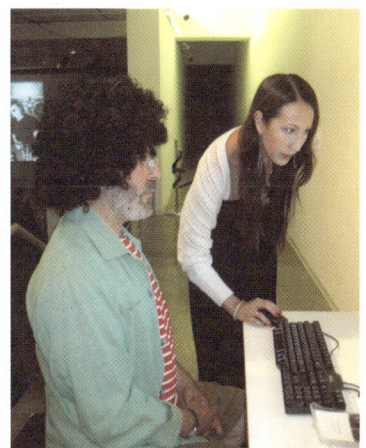

2012 Peter and Ava Shire

Donna has become the heart beat of the studio and the center of the Shire world: wife, mother, manager, facilitator, nurturer, hostess, and master problem-solver.

Peter clowning around with his daughter, Ava, during a computer session, wearing what has become his signature "gag"—a clown wig.

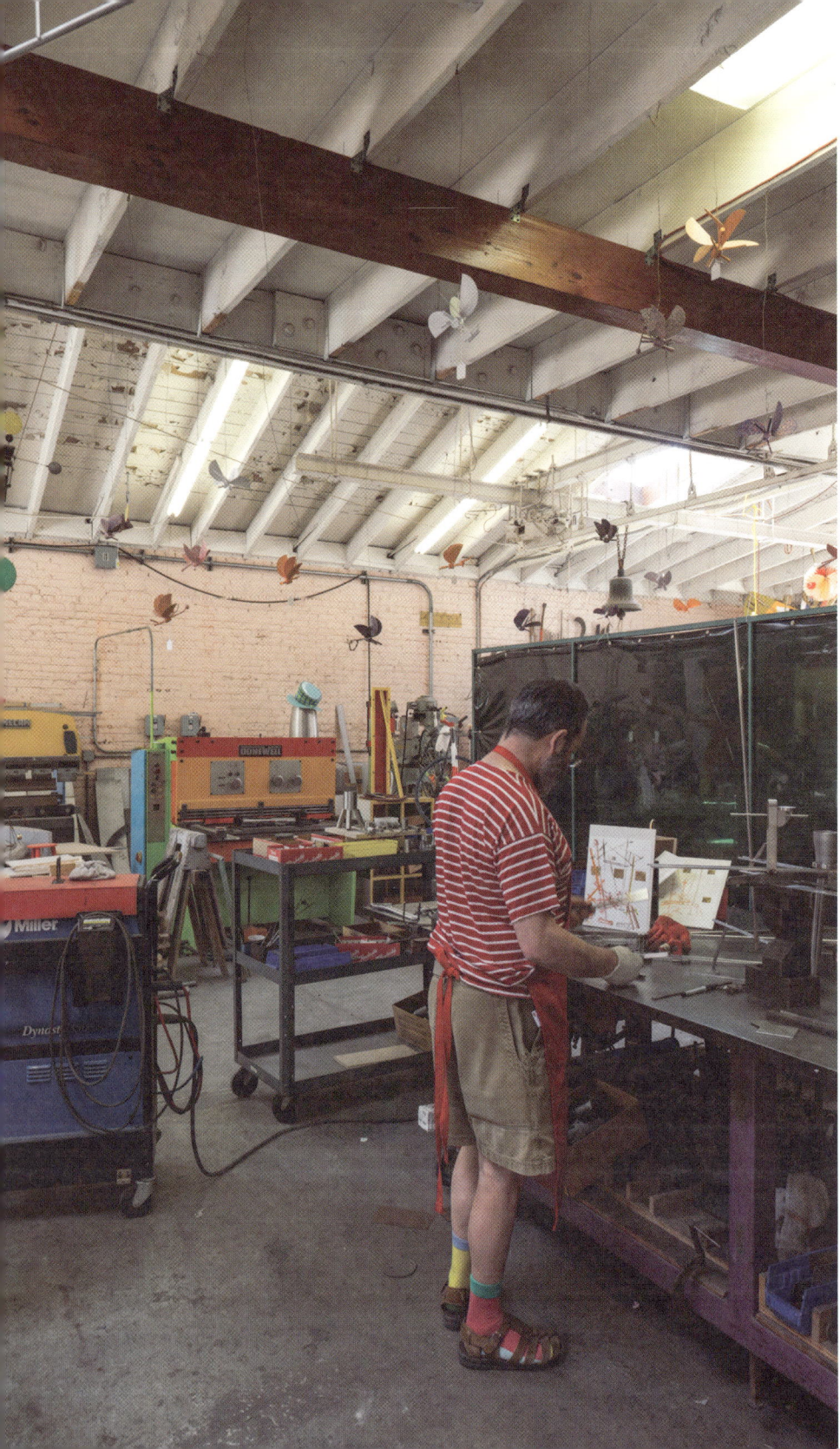

MEMPHIS MADE IN **CALIFORNIA—**
THREE STUDIO VISITS ACROSS TIME

By Darius A. Spieth

2012 Peter Shire in his Echo Park studio

> **If this exhibit sends any appreciable number of Americans to seek out the craftsmen of Italy in their home places, it will have justified itself. There are still untapped sources there, a steadily ripening mastery, a variety of production […] and in human encounters and picturesque experiences I assure you the search will be richly rewarding.[1]**

Almost five years after the end of World War II, in the spring of 1950, the Art Institute of Chicago, together with eleven other American museum institutions, organized a "field survey" of modern applied arts in Italy.[2] The effort would eventually culminate in the widely acclaimed *Italy at Work* traveling exhibition. One of the members of the exploratory committee sent over to Italy was the industrial designer Walter Dorwin Teague. Since the 1920s, Teague had established a reputation for revolutionizing the rolling stock of American railroad companies with his aerodynamic designs. In addition to countless designs of appliances, such as radios and cameras, he added a slick touch to the bodies of mid-century airplanes, conceived the softly flowing Art Deco roof lines of Texaco gas stations, and mounted Steinway pianos on bronze-sheathed legs evocative of skyscrapers. Almost single-handedly, Teague had invented the symbiosis of design and corporate identity in the American context. Industrial design was big business for him. Now, Italy came as a baffling revelation.

Teague and his colleagues visited the studios and workshops of architects, carpenters, glass blowers, and ceramicists. Uncompromisingly modern in design, the creations of their Italian counterparts were rooted in centuries-old crafts traditions, oftentimes influenced by local cultural customs. In Turin, there was Carlo Mollino's furniture created from plywood, bronze, and glass, which looked like aerodynamic dinosaurs. In Milan, the Americans encountered Gio Ponti's furniture and interiors defined by a biomorphic sobriety. In Florence, Guido Gambone's ceramics embraced the style of Picasso's Cubo-Surrealist medley, and on the island of Murano, near Venice, Alfredo Barbini shaped archaic forms out of molten glass. The designers and craftsmen worked more often than not out of makeshift workshops, and the destructions of the war were still visible everywhere. Despite the dreariness of the recent past, there was an ebullient sense of optimism, expressed through forms and color. The secret to the success of Italian design, then as now, was the close collaboration between architects, craftsmen, and industry.[3] Most surprising for Teague and his fellow travelers, however, was the realization that many of the Italian designers seemed to pursue their creative visions and experiments with a carefree disregard for the optimization of profits. Instead, what seemed to drive Italian designers was a quest for "heightened experience."[4]

Some forty years later, Italy afforded another American designer a revelation. This designer was Peter Shire. In the late 1970s, some of Shire's ceramics had appeared in *WET Magazine*, where they were seen by the architect Ettore Sottsass, a leading figure in the Italian design scene since the post-war years.[5] Sottsass was about to split from a designer collective called Studio Alchimia that had been founded in 1978 by Sandro Guerriero and Alessandro Mendini in order to launch his own design collaborative that would enter the history books as the Memphis group. Between 1981 and 1988, the original Milan-based association was sustained by the cabinetmaker Renzo Brugola and the entrepreneur Ernesto Gismondi, president of manufacturer Artemide. It would release annual collections of mostly furniture, but also comprising such things as glass and silver objects as well as textiles, which would define the postmodern style of the last two decades of the twentieth century.[6] Modeled on the conventions of the fashion world, the collections followed different themes, varying year by year, which found expression in the often evocative and exotic names given to the objects that the participating designers had contributed. In 1981, for instance, most objects were given names of world cities. Shire was a founding member of the group when he contributed to the inaugural collection of that year his geometricizing *Brazil* table (Fig. 1), followed in 1982 by the *Bel Air* chair (Pg. 24), the *Peninsula* table, and the *Anchorage* silver teapot (Fig. 2). Over subsequent years, the *Laurel* lamp (1985; Fig. 3) and the *Big Sur* sofa (1986) were added. At this point there was only one other American collaborator in the international group, the architect Michael Graves.

By calling itself Memphis, the group made a philosophical statement. The name referred both to Memphis in ancient Egypt and to Memphis, Tennessee—a landmark of American popular culture, home of Elvis Presley, and a pilgrimage site for rock 'n' roll enthusiasts:

> **The name Memphis must have come up on the evening of December 11 [1980] at Sottsass's house. There was a Bob Dylan record on, *Stuck inside of Mobile with the Memphis**

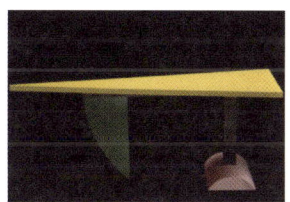

Fig. 1 Peter Shire, *Brazil Table*, 1981 Memphis Collection, wood and lacquer. 205 x 80 x 72 cm.

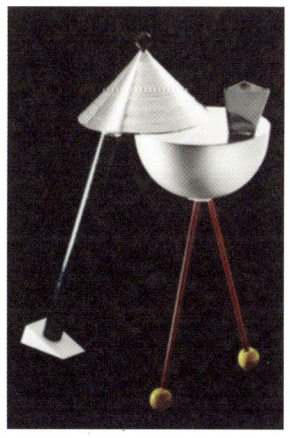

Fig. 2 Peter Shire, *Anchorage Teapot*, 1982 Memphis Collection, silver and silver-plated metal. 40 cm (height).

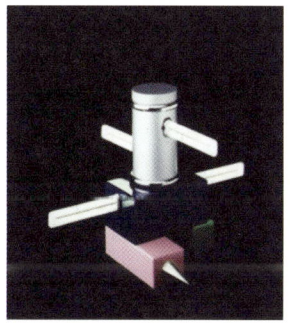

Fig. 3 Peter Shire, *Laurel Lamp*, 1985 Memphis Collection, metal, aluminum, and neon tubing. 42 x 34 x 29 cm.

Blues Again, and since nobody bothered to change the record, Bob Dylan went on howling *the Memphis blues again,* until Sottsass said, "o.k., let's call it Memphis," and everybody thought it was a great name: Blues, Tennessee, rock 'n' roll, American suburbs, and then Egypt, the Pharaohs' capital, the city of the god Ptah.[7] **"**

The fusing or "double-coding"—an expression coined in the late 1970s by Charles Jencks, the principal theoretician of postmodern architectural theory—of "high" and "low" cultural elements would become a defining theme on the agenda of the Memphis project.[8] Translated into the material terms of furniture design, this hybridity expressed itself most poignantly in the juxtaposition of "cheap" (but colorful) plastic laminates such as one would encounter, for instance, in fast food restaurants, with "expensive-looking" (but in fact low-cost) veneers made of African woods, as seen in Sottsass's sideboard *Tartar* (Fig. 4) or Aldo Cibic's writing desk *Sophia* (Fig. 5), both from the 1985 Memphis collection.[9] There was also a distinct preference for zigzag patterns, asymmetry, and visual shorthands of all kinds, referencing electronic circuit boards and the coming of the computer age. Other pieces of furniture, defying the dictates of functionalism, integrated such oddities as light bulbs and

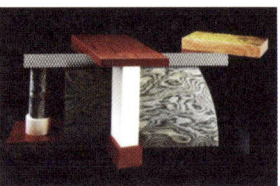

Fig. 4 Ettore Sottsass, *Tartar Sideboard,* 1985 Memphis Collection, wood, imitation wood veneer, and plastic laminate. 19 x 85 x 78 cm.

imitation snake skin (Fig. 6)—visual puns that more often than not made only the initiate chuckle (and left everyone else baffled).[10] But even a superficial observer could not avoid the realization that Memphis objects were all about humor and irony. If Memphis design were a person confronted with the question "Are you serious?," the answer would be that it is very serious about not being serious. (Those who know Peter Shire personally will immediately understand that this attitude greatly contributed to the synergies between him and the Memphis project.) Undoubtedly, there was a certain snobbism inherent in the very concept of Memphis. Despite the connotations of "cheapness" implied by some of the materials selected, the objects were never produced on anything like an industrial scale. They were carefully handcrafted—mostly on demand for the more ambitious items—and catered to a small and sophisticated market of design enthusiasts. In this sense, they serve as high-end cultural signifiers literally hiding under a veneer of allusions to mass culture and industrial production methods.

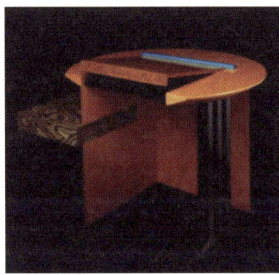

Fig. 5 Aldo Cibic, *Sophia Writing Desk,* 1985 Memphis Collection, wood, briar and imitation wood veneer, and lacquer. 120 x 90 x 75 cm.

In 1979, Sottsass sent fellow designers Matteo Thun and Aldo Cibic to Los Angeles to work with Peter Shire on a group of articles for the Italian magazine

Casa Vogue. One of the first things Shire noticed about the visitors when they showed up at the doorstep of his studio in Echo Park was that they wore "great shoes." As they parted, Matteo Thun, in a foreboding voice, announced: "You *must* come to Milan. *This is your moment.*" Indeed, it was Shire's calling. He had never traveled to Europe before, and a few months later he was on his way to Milan. Thun and Cibic hosted him during his stay, which also afforded Shire the opportunity to meet Marco Zanini, Michele de Lucchi, Barbara Radice, George Sowden, and Nathalie du Pasquier. Already the transit from the airport to the city proved to be exciting. Shire noticed in passing junk yards filled with the mangled carcasses of "every car he had ever wanted to have in high school": Citroëns, Alfa Romeos, Fiats, or Lancias. The experience of working with the Italian artists could best be characterized as creative chaos, but one located in design heaven. There was a true *esprit de corps*, and members of the group showed genuine interest in each other's work; dialogue was an inherent element in the group dynamics. The experience of his first visit to Studio Alchimia's headquarters located in the basement of an Art Nouveau building at 55 Foro Buonaparte "charmed" Shire "beyond words." The underground gathering place of the designers, which struck him as an "alchemist's den," was accessible only through a somber patio that was tucked away in the interior courtyard of the building. On this occasion, he met Sandro Guerriero and then Andrea Branzi, another founding member of the Memphis group. Branzi's ruffled appearance à la Jacques Tati and his habit of carrying small "bottle-like objects" that weighed down his coat pockets reminded Shire of a "wino," until at one point Branzi revealed the objects, which turned out to be his hallmark weather vane sculptures. Later on, when he was invited to lunch at the Branzis, he discovered to his amazement a geometricized teapot constructed only from three blue tubes arranged at an angle, which previously he had only seen in illustrations. The meal itself turned into an unexpected cultural challenge, since Shire did not know how to eat spaghetti properly. Despite the warm welcome, the organizational deficiencies of the Alchimia enterprise were blatantly obvious. The people running it, as Shire puts it, "could never quite tie their shoes."

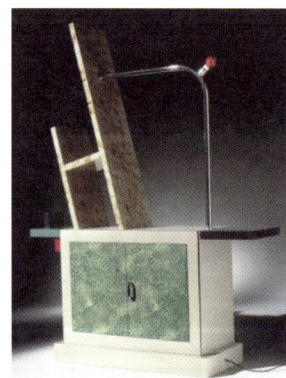

Shire had arrived at a moment when the breakaway of the Memphis group from Studio Alchimia was imminent. Many future members of Memphis perceived a "macabre" side in Mendini, because, as Shire recalled, he maintained "that nothing new could be done." Indeed, Mendini would write in his *Alchimia Manifesto* of July 1985 that "design is a cycle: everything that will have to happen has already happened. [...] Design is delicate and does not impose itself, but stays beside and gently accompanies the lives and deaths of the people who like it."[11] Memphis never published a manifesto, but Ettore Sottsass and his followers wanted to create design that was innovative, forceful, and optimistic.

Fig. 6 Ettore Sottsass, *Beverly Sideboard,* 1981 Memphis Collection, wood, briar, and imitation snake skin veneer, plastic laminate, chrome-plated steel, and light bulb. 175 x 48 x 228 cm.

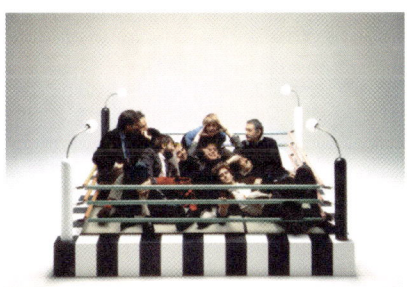

Fig. 7 Masanori Umeda, *Tawaraya Boxing Ring*, 1981
Memphis Collection, wood, metal, straw mats, plastic
laminate, light bulbs. 280 x 280 x 120 cm. In the ring,
from the left: Aldo Cibic, Andrea Branzi, Michele De Lucchi,
Marco Zanini, Nathalie Du Pasquier, George Sowden, Martine
Bedin, Matteo Thun, Ettore Sottsass.

Despite the label of postmodernism that subsequently became attached to the group, the aesthetic positions of its practitioners followed the classical lines of the historical avant-garde of the early twentieth century. From Shire's perspective, the emphasis on the collaboration between art and industry in particular reminded him of the premises of the German Bauhaus in the 1920s. Like for the Bauhaus, the mission was to increase the quality of people's lives through truthful design. Appropriately for this philosophy, Thun once remarked during a conversation that "Memphis was way ahead of its time," to which Shire, inverting the temporal thrust, replied that "it always will be." Sottsass, who struck Shire as "aggressive" in the uncompromising pursuit of his aesthetic goals, said that the tools of his father, who had worked as an architect in Innsbruck, Austria, were "pen, ruler, and pencil," whereas his was "the airplane." The statement alludes to both the dictum of early twentieth-century Russian Constructivist designer-engineer Alexander Rodchenko, who affirmed that all of his graphic art was created by using only "rulers, compass, and drawing pens," and the obsession with airplanes of the Italian Futurists under the leadership of Filippo Tommaso Marinetti.[12] Within the more immediate context of the Memphis group, however, Sottsass must have thought primarily of his goal to bring together a truly globalized group of designers (Fig. 7). Both he and Thun had strong ties to Austria. They were joined by Nathalie du Pasquier from France and George Sowden from Great Britain, as well as Masanori Umeda and Shiro Kuramata from Japan. Not only were the designers and the names of the objects in the collections international, but so was the aesthetic appeal of the products themselves. Within less than four years Memphis design became an international success story, sold through representative offices across North America, Western Europe, and even places as remote as Brazil, Lebanon, South Africa, and Australia.[13] It is against the backdrop of the transnational reach of the group that one must perceive Shire's involvement with Memphis. His career stands symptomatically for the rise and worldwide recognition of art and design from Southern California during the second half of the twentieth century.

An afternoon visit to Peter Shire's studio in L.A.'s Echo Park neighborhood is a memorable event. More than thirty years after the visit by Matteo Thun and Aldo Cibic, I retraced their steps in June 2012. The Shire Studios had since relocated, but only a short distance—to larger premises housed in what was originally built in 1925 as an automotive garage (Fig. 8). The visit came almost as an afterthought, on the last day of a six-month visiting professorship at Caltech. I had seen Peter Shire's sculptures from the Hokkaido series a few weeks earlier in a one-man show at his

brother's La Luz de Jesus Gallery, and the experience had rekindled my teenage passion for Memphis design.[14] Unexpectedly, I found myself in the backyard of the Memphis group's Californian outpost—Peter Shire's great American design playground on Echo Park Avenue. Golden sunlight bathed the pastel-colored façades of homes from the 1920s and 1930s lining the gentle slope of the street as it branches off Sunset Boulevard. Mexican voices and music emanating from the interior courtyards of an occasional apartment building filled the air. Street signage and mural paintings reflected the visual and ethnic diversity of the neighborhood.

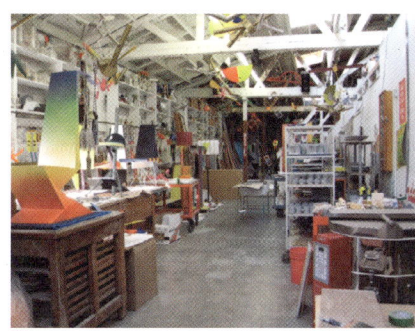

Fig. 8 Peter Shire Studios on Echo Park Avenue, Los Angeles.

Then there were the Peter Shire Studios themselves, recessed from the street, yet clearly demarcated by outsized and brightly colored outdoor sculptures that seemed to have been casually deposited in the courtyard of a defunct industrial plant. I found Peter Shire and some of his collaborators busy at work constructing a small piece of pottery, whose distinctly architectural appearance reminded me immediately of work by the Memphis group. While Peter built the object, his wife Donna gave me a tour of the facilities, which turned out to be much larger than anything I had expected. There were long rows of shelves with completed ceramic pieces everywhere along the walls, as well as kilns and welding equipment for making furniture and steel sculptures. A back room was filled with Shire-designed Murano glass from the late 1980s, the result of another "Italian job" sponsored this time by the owner of Vistosi glassworks, Mauro Albarelli, and an endless number of slide folders documenting the artist's many projects over the years.[15] The welding shop contained pieces of furniture in various stages of completion, including a reproduction of a table designed during the 1980s in the Memphis style (but not part of one of the collections themselves), which was a recent private commission from a collector in Germany. The lure of the Memphis style had apparently remained undiminished thirty years later. At the end of the tour, I was allowed to climb an old wooden ladder to take a peek into the storage area under the roof of the former garage, and a seemingly endless sea of packaged Shire objects unfolded before my eyes. It was this vision perhaps more than anything else that provided the impetus for the three-venue survey at LSU documented in this catalog.

The conversation with the artist following the tour turned very soon to the subject of the Echo Park neighborhood and its distinct cultural flavor. Shire was born in Echo Park and has lived there all his life. Some of his ancestors arrived with the Californian Gold Rush in the 1860s, and his father was a card-carrying Communist house builder, carpenter, and union activist during the late 1930s and 1940s. Many modernist L.A. homes designed by architect Rudolf Schindler, a former collaborator of Frank Lloyd

Wright, were "physically kept standing" with the help of Henry Shire. Over time, the Echo Park neighborhood unfailingly attracted individualists, artists, and writers, often with liberal and counter-cultural leanings. William Faulkner lived in Echo Park, along with Art Pepper, Ed Ruscha, Paul Landacre, Mack Sennett, Woody Guthrie, William S. Hart, and Carey McWilliams. Another Austrian-born architect besides Schindler, Richard Neutra, defined Southern California's mid-century modernism from here. The movie industry and Hollywood were always part of both the local culture and the economy. Several films were named after the neighborhood, which served as a set on numerous occasions – most famously perhaps for *Chinatown*, Roman Polanski's Oscar-winning neo-noir drama from 1974. Many actors, such as Anthony Quinn, Steve McQueen, and Leonardo DiCaprio lived at least for some time in Echo Park. From very early on, however, the freewheeling lifestyle also had its discontents. In 1923, the pioneer radio-evangelist Aimee Semple McPherson built the first megachurch in Echo Park, called the Angelus Temple. Although McPherson was never at loss for words when it came to branding the moral corruption of the city, she used Hollywood-style special effects for her sermons, which included such elements as speaking in tongues and miracle healings. As Shire noted with a chuckle, she would later be parodied by British writer Evelyn Waugh in the fictional character Aimée Thanatogenos. Waugh's Aimée appeared as a funerary cosmetician in the novel *The Loved One*, a very noir piece of L.A. literature about the tragicomical love affair between two embalmers working on pets and humans, respectively. In fact, even from the Shire Studios, L.A. noir is never very far. In 1943, the racially-motivated Zoot Suit Riots, pitting Mexican Americans against military servicemen, erupted near the Marine Naval Reserve in Echo Park itself, about a mile west of where the Shires live and work today.

the Memphis style (Fig. 9). The gallery was started in 1971 on Melrose Avenue by Billy Shire and his mother, and was then called the Soap Plant, in reference to the principal merchandise, soap and baskets.[17] It was just the first in a series of stores with exotic names and even more exotic offerings that would soon be frequented by celebrities such as Dave and Patricia Arquette, Nicolas Cage, Johnny Depp, and Michael Jackson. As a former director of La Luz de Jesus, Robert Lopez (El Vez), recalled,

> **La Luz de Jesus was a natural extension of the 'Soap Plant Idea.' The art of soaps, ceramics, books, and world culture was the Soap Plant. The art of toys, design, fake poo, and bad taste was Wacko. The art of fashion and fabrics in ethnic and pop culture was Zulu. To me, La Luz de Jesus was the intersection of all these stores, with the brazen and, of course, justified gall to label and present it as Art with a capital 'A.'[18]**

Of the hundreds of artists represented by La Luz de Jesus over the years, one finds some of the most iconic figures of the Lowbrow art scene, including Ed "Big Daddy" Roth, George Barris, the Clayton Brothers, Joe Coleman, Coop, Manuel Ocampo, Gary Panter, The Pizz, Mark Ryden, and Robert Williams, founder of *Juxtapoz* magazine.[19] Mixed in with this eclectic group, there were always exhibitions of Peter Shire's work, distinctive because of its clear, geometric forms. The aesthetics of La Luz de Jesus share with Memphis not only the love of pop culture in all its forms, but also many affinities on the level of formal qualities. Probably the most iconic artworks that emerged from the Lowbrow art movement in the 1980s and 1990s were the paintings by Robert Williams, which often featured bright primary colors and aggressively overlaid patterns similar to Memphis furniture designs (Fig. 10). Williams, however, was not aware of the existence of the Milanese group at the time.[20] It was because of Ettore

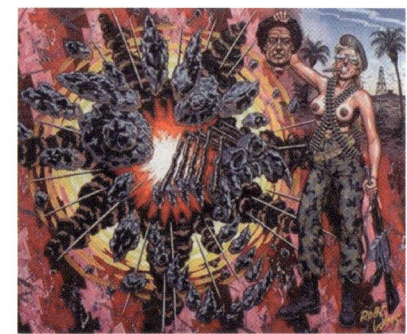

Fig. 10 Robert Williams, *Coup d'Etat Totem*, ca. 1987, oil on canvas. 48 x 61 cm. Private collection.

Sottsass's sensitivity to these affinities, from thousands of miles away, that Peter Shire was invited to become a member of Memphis. This collaboration established a link between two different design worlds, which would otherwise never have gotten to know each other.

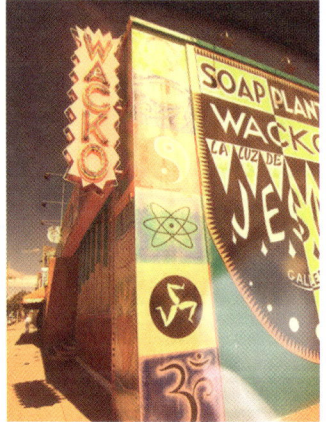

Fig. 9 Billy Shire's *La Luz de Jesus Gallery* on Hollywood Boulevard, Los Angeles.

One connection that has been almost consistently overlooked in the context of Shire's Memphis style is the parallel with the rise of the L.A. Lowbrow art scene. The reason for this omission is mostly a question of chronology: Memphis is commonly associated with the glitzier side of 1980s European design, Lowbrow with grungy 1990s California underground culture (comics, hot rods, pulp novels, tattoos, graffiti, etc.). How could these two extremes possibly fit together? The missing link between them is Peter's brother Billy Shire, an inveterate collector of folk art and director of La Luz de Jesus Gallery on Hollywood Boulevard, who has been nicknamed the "Peggy Guggenheim of Lowbrow."[16] Although different in temperament, the two brothers continue to have close ties; their houses in Echo Park face each other across an empty lot. Even the brightly colored murals and spiky, painted decorations of La Luz de Jesus's façade—a converted former post office building—look like a psychedelic version of

Even if Shire's art in all its forms—furniture, ceramics, glass, sculpture, or drawing— captures something of the colors, the exuberance, and the rhythm of life in Echo Park, it does transcend local boundaries and cultural contexts. With their strictly geometric formal vocabulary, many of his creations cite the abstract Utopian designs of the Russian avant-garde from the early twentieth century, epitomized by the designers, engineers, and all-purpose monteurs of the Suprematist and Constructivist movements, such as Kaslmlr Malevlch, El Lissitzky, Vladimir Tatlin, and Alexander Rodchenko. There is also a good dose of the Futurists' fascination with the notion of speed inherent in his designs. Shire's work updates these artists' vision to account for the cultural and social changes operative at the turn of the twenty-first century, such as multiculturalism, postmodernism, globalization, consumerism, the rise of computer technology, or even the search for alternative forms of consciousness. For all of these explorations, Los Angeles remains one of the great laboratories.

The very fact that Shire was invited more than thirty years ago to join the Memphis group is, with hindsight, a symptom of the global rise of the L.A. art scene. The emergence of L.A. as an art hub of global stature was extensively documented between October 2011 and April 2012 by the Pacific Standard Time initiative of the Getty. It involved more than sixty art institutions across Southern California, which, mostly through retrospective exhibitions, celebrated "the birth of the L.A. art scene," when the city "experienced its cultural coming of age" and "local artists suddenly became global artists."[21] The Pacific Standard Time events covered the period between 1945 and 1980, that is, they stopped at precisely the moment when Peter Shire's Memphis story begins. The fascinating history of the depth and richness of L.A. creativity in the visual arts during the 1980s and 1990s, including Memphis-style design and Lowbrow art, thus still remains in large part to be written. By presenting an overview of the artist who helped turn the L.A. style into a global phenomenon over the course of roughly one generation, from 1980 to 2012, the current retrospective exhibitions of Peter Shire's work intend to provide one possible starting point for the study of what came after the "birth of the L.A. art scene."[22]

Darius A. Spieth, PhD
Associate Professor of Art History
LSU School of Art

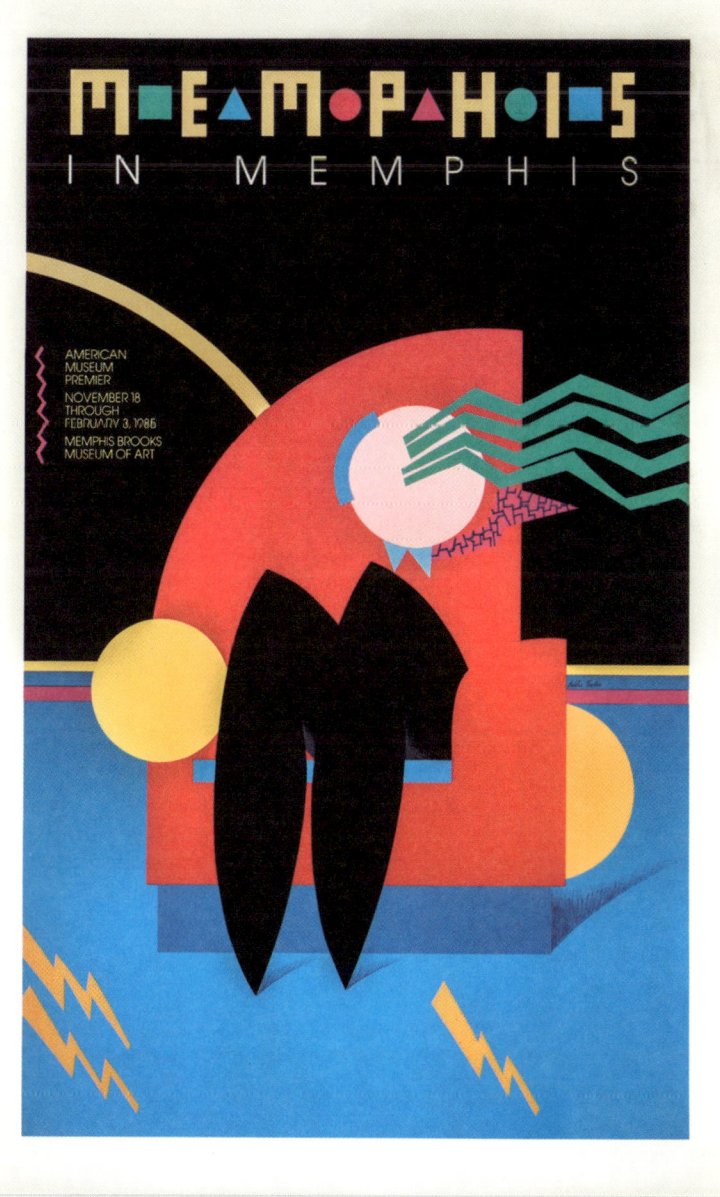

MEMPHIS, Poster, 1985, 27.25 x 17.75", Framed, Print

ENDNOTES

1 Walter Dorwin Teague, "Foreword," in Meyric R. Rogers, *Italy at Work: Her Renaissance in Design Today* (Rome: Compagnia Nazionale Artigiana, 1950), 11.

2 Ibid., 16.

3 Albrecht Bangert, *Italienisches Möbeldesign: Klassiker von 1945 bis 1985* (Munich: Bangert Verlag, 1985), 13.

4 Observation by Peter Shire from an e-mail exchange with the author, December 5, 2012.

5 Telephone interview by the author with Peter Shire, Oct. 24, 2012.

6 Barbara Radice, *Memphis: Research, Experiences, Results, Failures and Success of New Design* (New York: Rizzoli, 1984), 26.

7 Ibid. As a coda to the "classical" Memphis collections of the years 1981 to 1988, the Meta-Memphis and Post-Design collections were launched beginning in 1989. I am excluding these designs, which had a much more limited importance, from the current discussion because of their difference in style and creators involved.

8 Charles Jencks, *The Language of Post-Modern Architecture*, rev. ed. (1977; reprint, London: Academy Edition, 1981), 6, 8, 90, 116, 130-31, 146.

9 These wood-grain veneers were manufactured by Legno Alpi (Alpi Woods), based in Modigliana, near Bologna, and were specifically treated to fit the Memphis look. Hence, the veneers are also referred to as Alpi veneers.

10 All plastic veneers, such as the imitation snake skin, were designed by Ettore Sottsass, George Sowden, or Michele de Lucchi. They were custom-made by Abet Laminati.

11 Alessandro Mendini, "The Alchimia Manifesto," in *Alchimia: Never-Ending Italian Design*, ed. Kazuko Sato (Tokyo: Rikuyo-sha Publishing, 1985), 7.

12 *Alexander Rodchenko: Spatial Constructions* (Ostfildern-Ruit: Hatje Cantz, 2002), 16, 27-28; Bruno Mantura, Patrizia Rosazza Ferraris, and Livia Velani, *Futurism in Flight: "Aeropittura" Paintings and Sculptures of Man's Conquest of Space, 1913-1945* (Rome: De Luca, 1990).

13 *Memphis Milano*, trade catalog (Milan, ca. 1985), 88.

14 On the Hokkaido Series, see Peter Shire, *Hokkaido Story: California—Sapporo Steel Sculpture & Ikebana Teapot Forms* (Los Angeles: La Luz de Jesus Gallery, 2011), as well as the illustrations in this catalogue.

15 On the collaboration with Vistosi, see Lisa Hammel, "In 3 Craft Shows, Color and Joy," in *The New York Times*, February 9, 1989. See also the exhibition catalog of these glass objects, *Ponte Vivarini, Palazzo Series: Peter Shire* (Venice/Mestre: Foligraf, 1998).

16 John Gunnin, "The Shire Empire: LA Style Magnates," *Juxtapoz* 2, no. 2 (Spring 1996): 47.

17 Ibid.

18 Statement by Robert Lopez, in *La Luz de Jesus 25: The Little Gallery That Could*, ed. Janice S. Gore (Los Angeles: La Luz de Jesus Press, 2011), 4.

19 See also the roster of artists included in *La Luz de Jesus 25: The Little Gallery That Could*.

20 Interview by the author with Robert Williams during the artist's visit to the LSU campus, November 12, 2012. Peter Shire, in turn, was keenly aware of Robert Williams' work, because Peter's brother Billy represented Robert Williams over extended periods.

21 *Pacific Standard Time: Los Angeles Art, 1945-1980*, ed. Rebecca Peabody et al. (Los Angeles: Getty Research Institute, 2011). The quotations were taken from the promotional video accompanying the Pacific Standard Time events: http://www.pacificstandardtime.org/videos (Pacific Standard Time Anthem).

22 As evidence for the global recognition and impact of Peter Shire's design by the end of the 1980s, one can cite, for example, the following discussion of his work that a leading German interior design magazine commissioned from Ed Ruscha, "Design Guide to High Style Los Angeles/Design, Architektur, Restaurants, Shopping: Los Angeles," *Architektur & Wohnen*, 1/1990 (February/March 1990): 106.

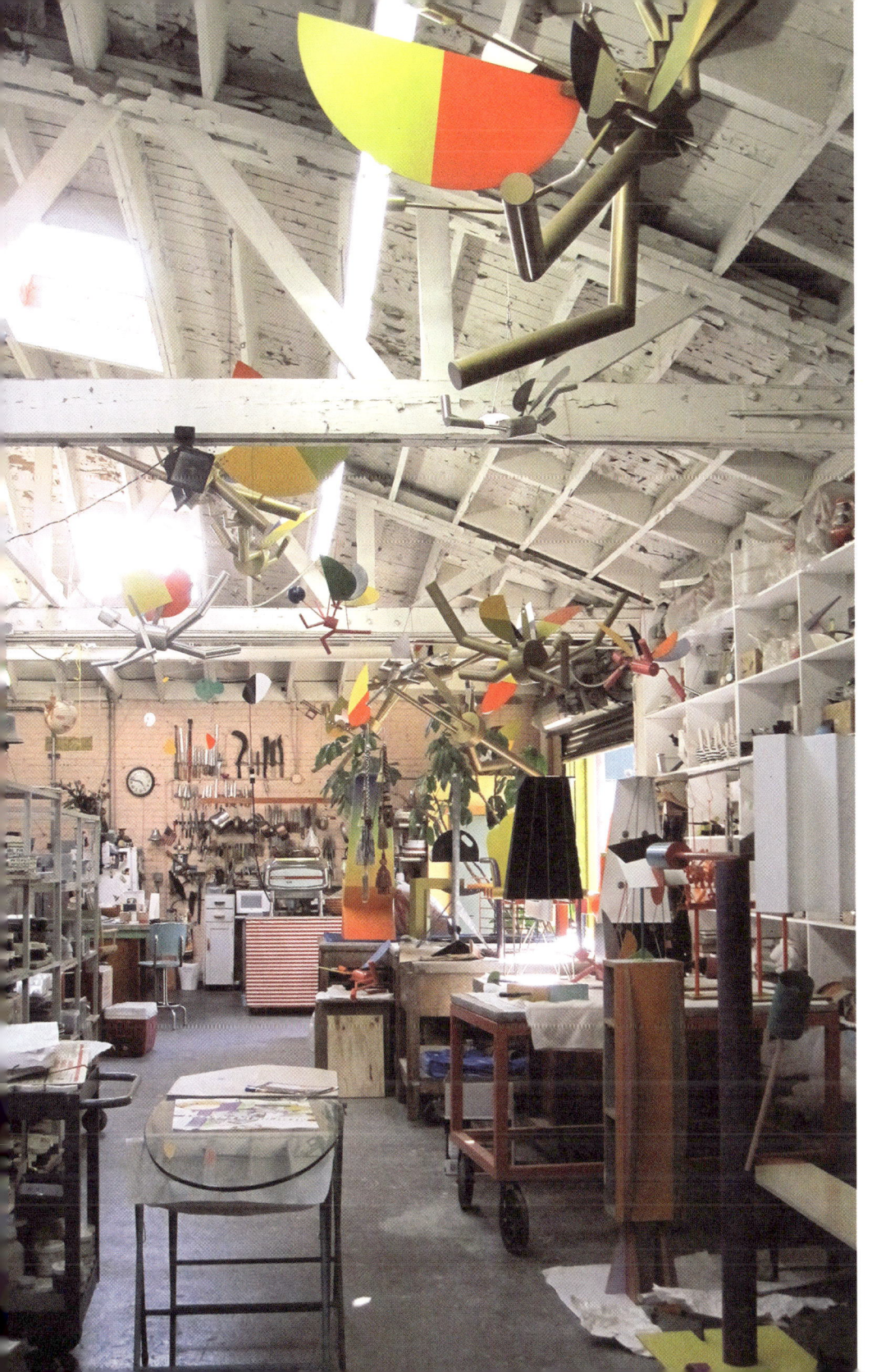

PETER SHIRE:
ONE RETROSPECTIVE, THREE VENUES

LSU Museum of Art • LSU School of Art Glassell Gallery • LSU Union Art Gallery

2012 Peter Shire studio

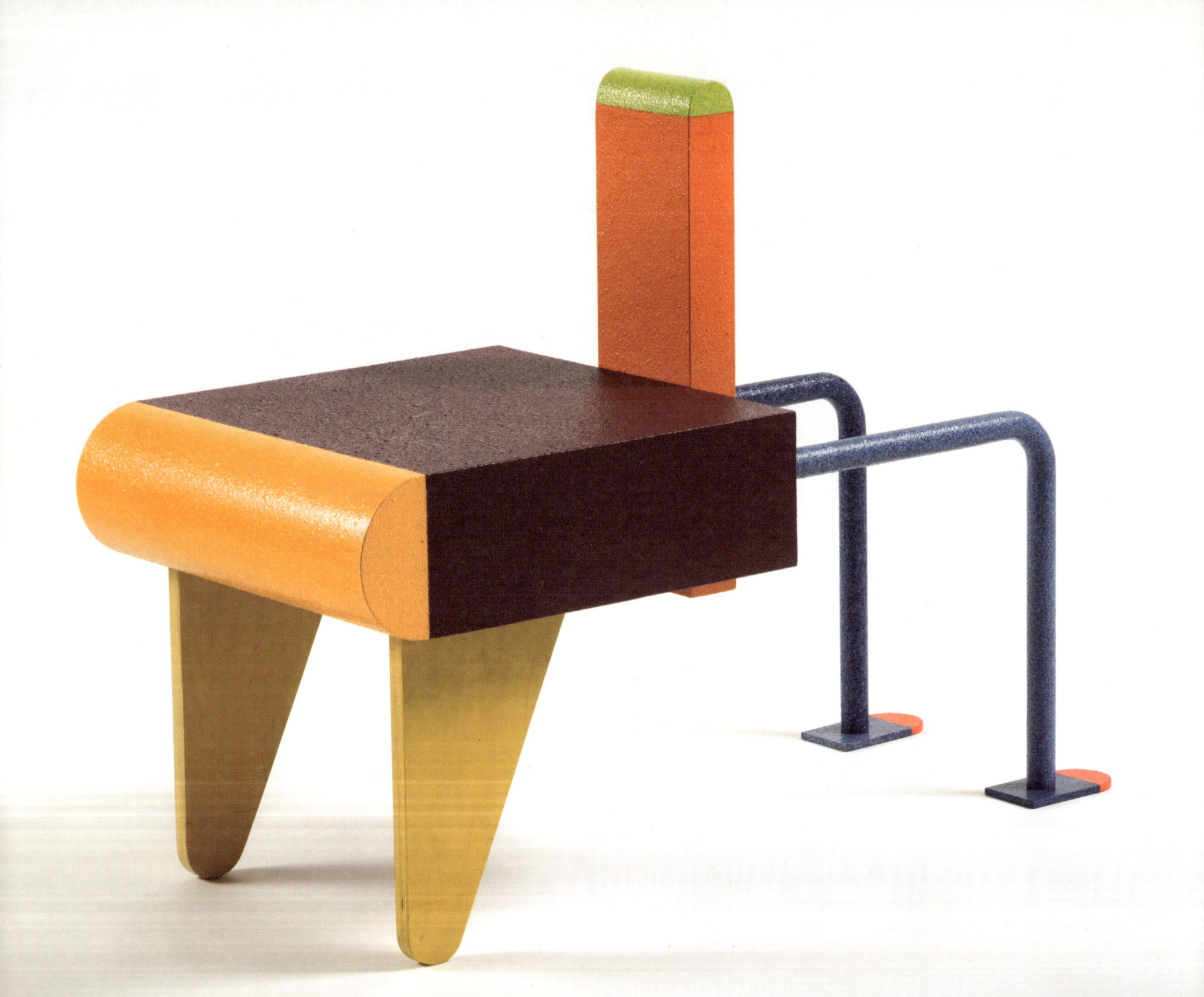

LSU Museum of Art

Practically Absurd:
Art & Design by Peter Shire

Bete Longe, Chair, 2007, 26" x 34.5" x 16", Steel, enamel

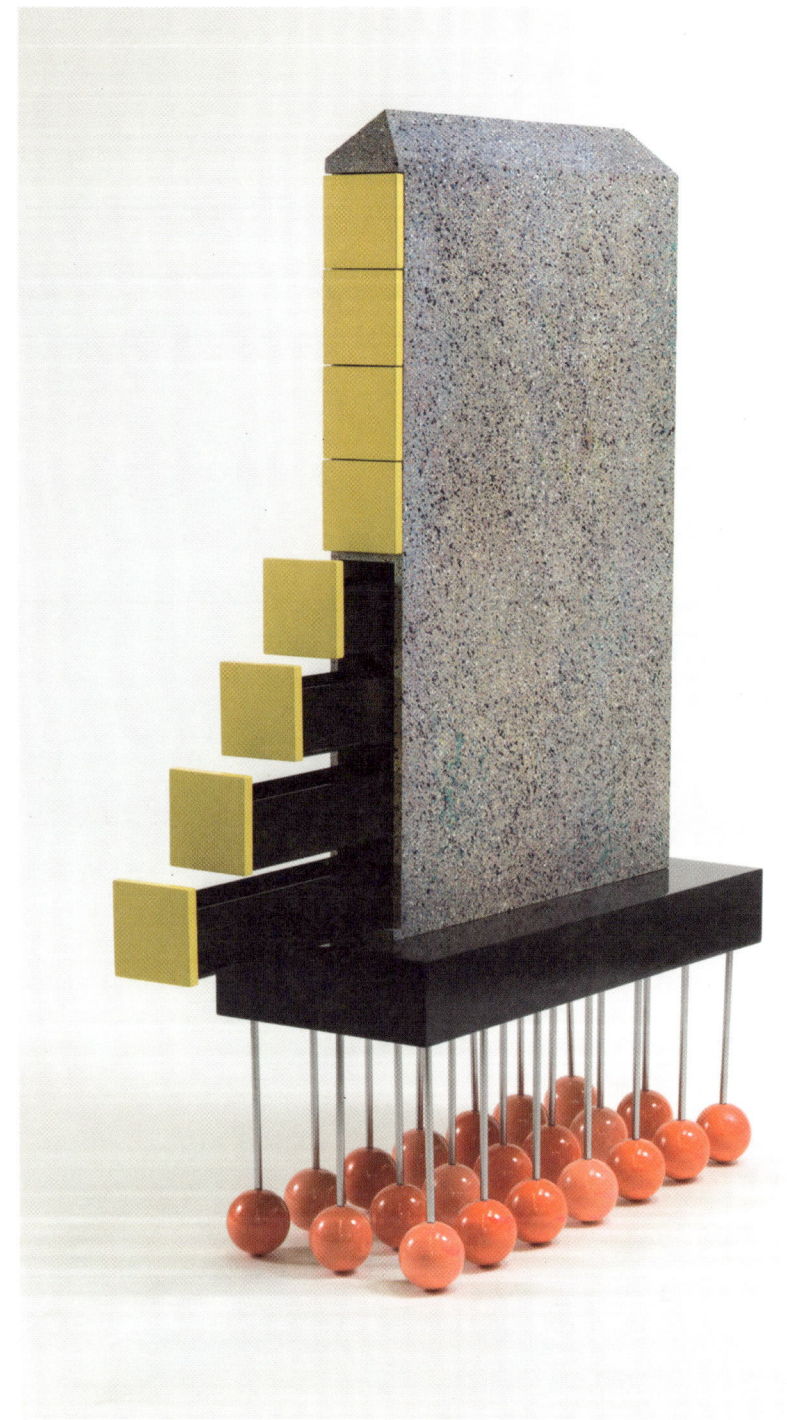

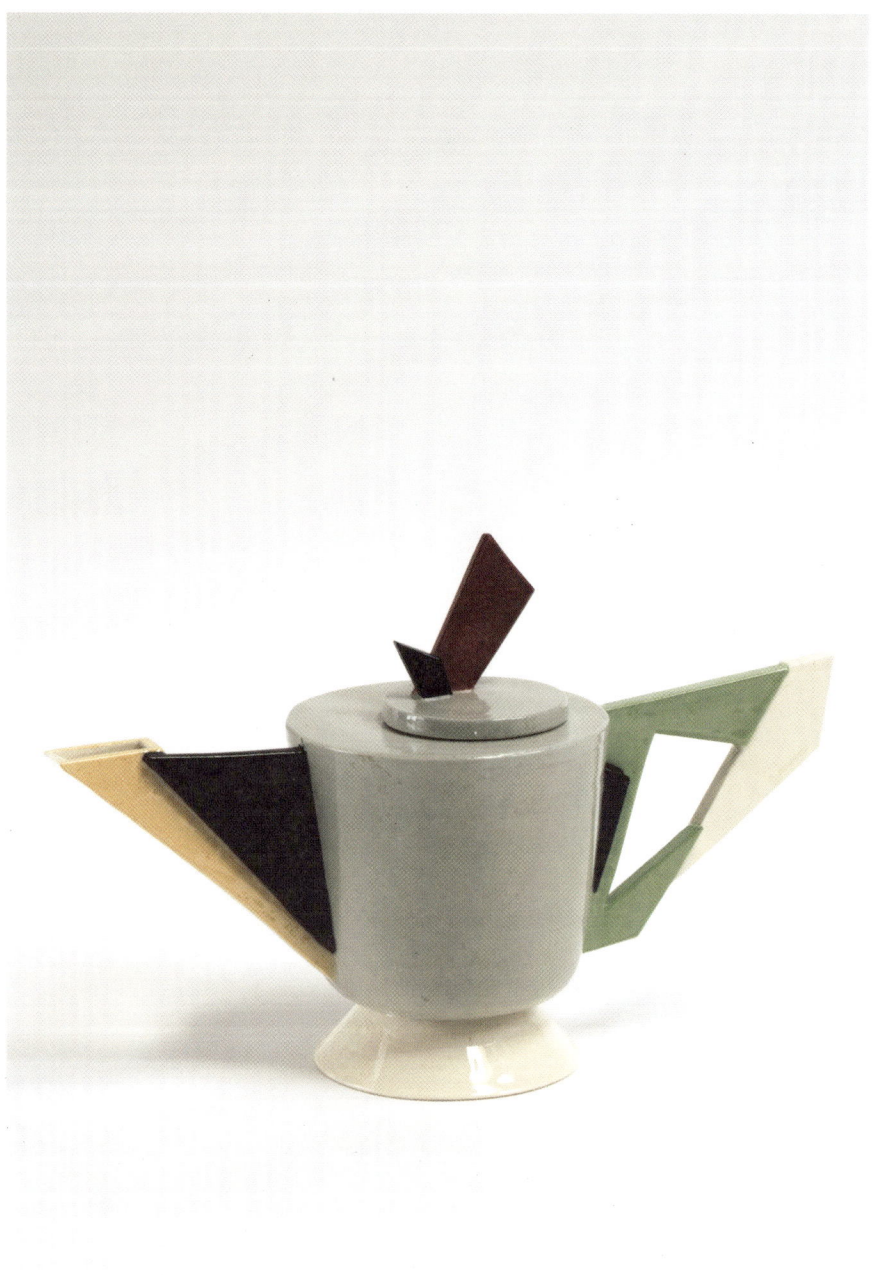

Obelisk, Drawer, 1981, 69" x 40.5" x 16.5", Wood, steel, chrome, enamel

Jazz Modern, Teapot, c.1980, 8.5" x 13.25" x 5.25", Ceramic

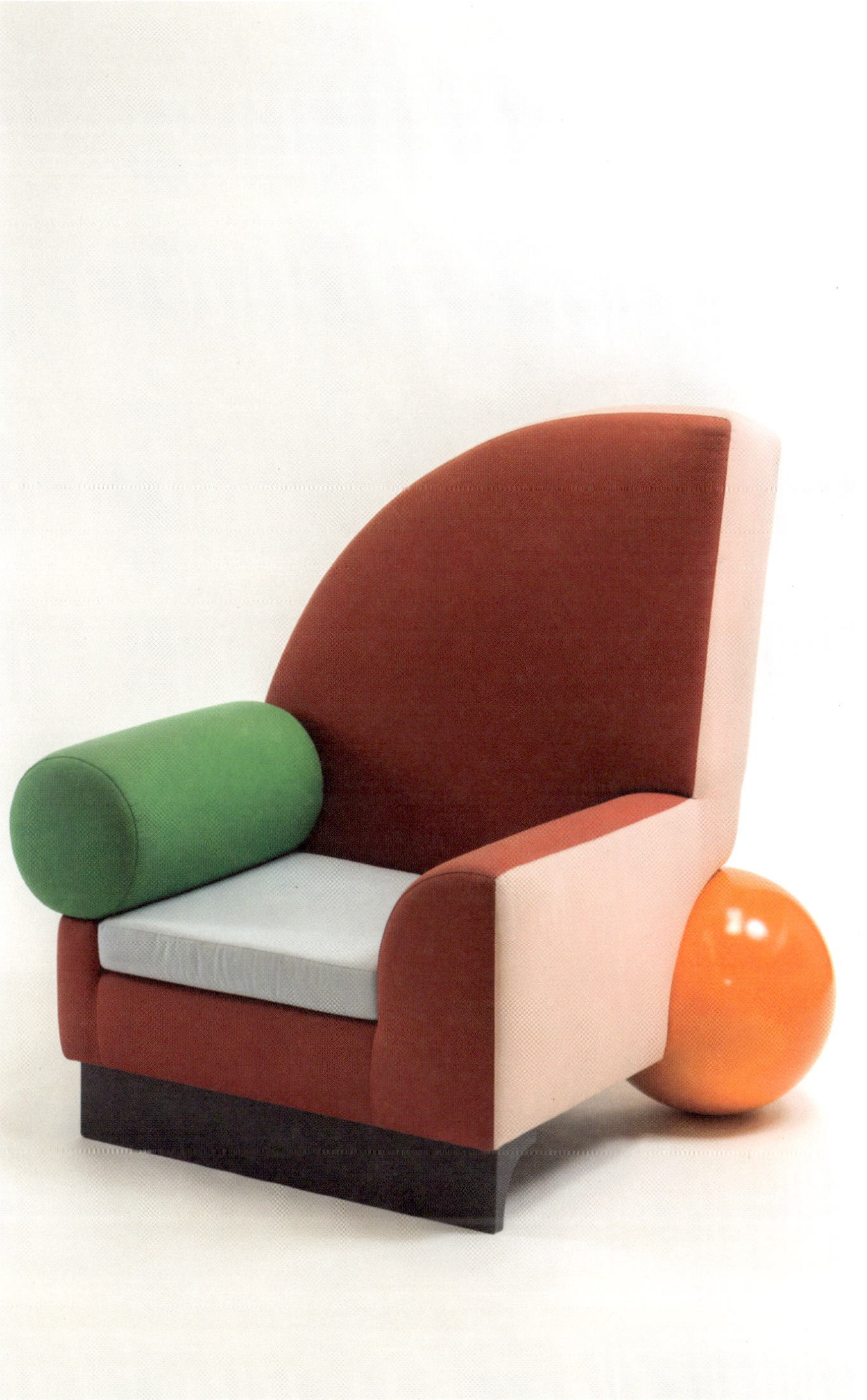

Bel Air, Chair, MEMPHIS, 1981, 48.5" x 43" x 48.5", Wood, steel, upholstery fabric

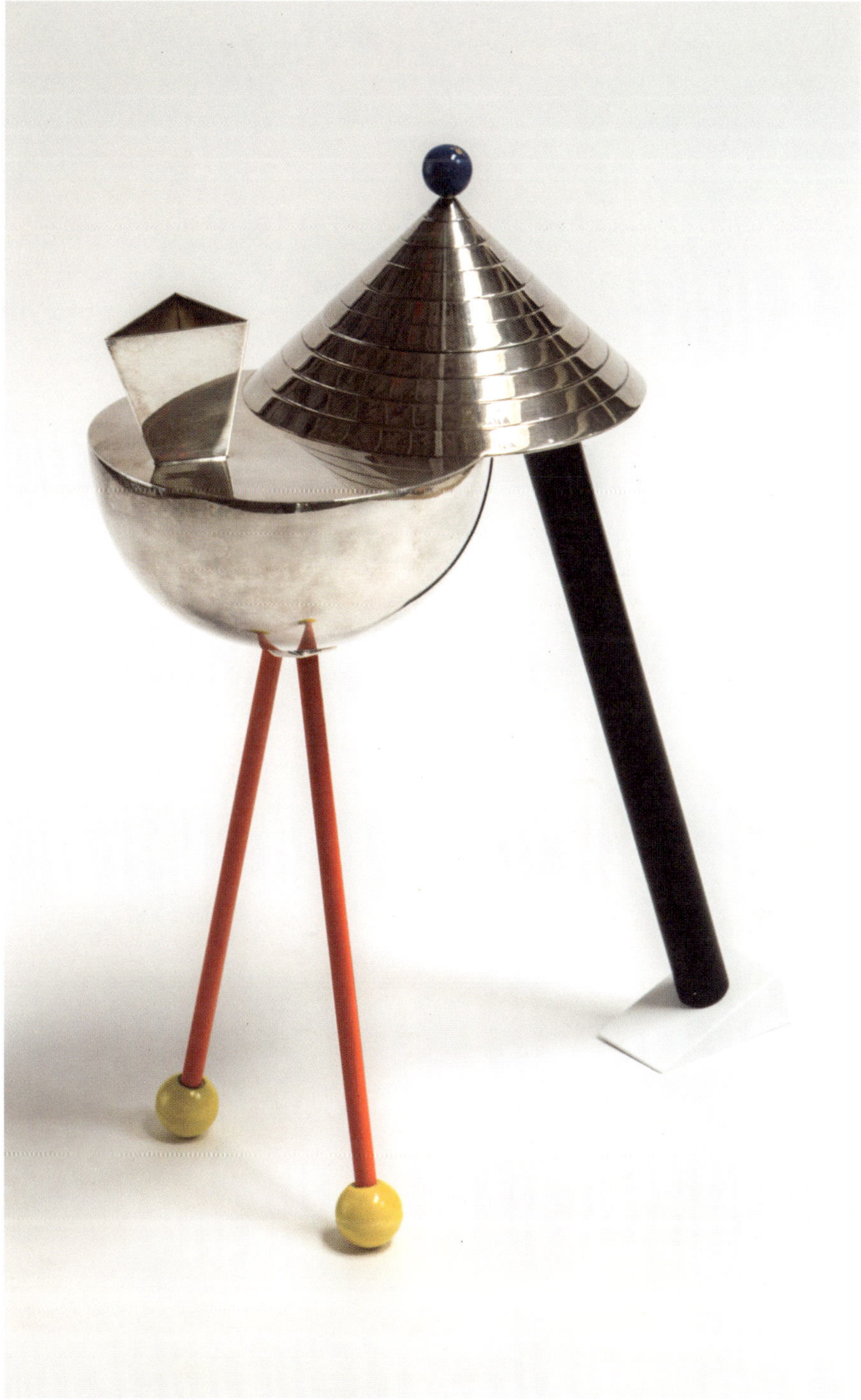

Anchorage, Teapot, MEMPHIS, 1983, 15" x 12.75" x 5.75", Silver, wood enamel

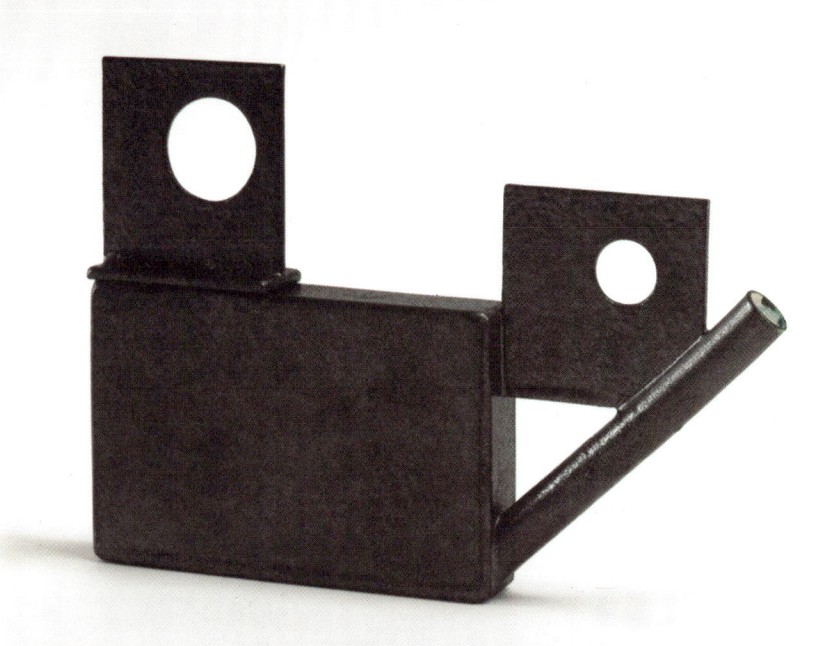

Saki Negri, Pot, 1980, 6.25" x 8.5" x 1", Ceramic

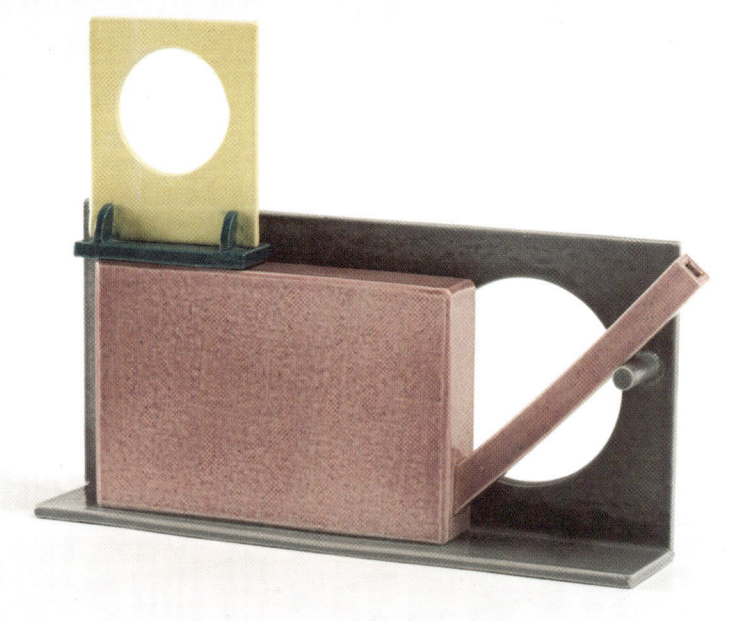

Saki Rosa, Pot, 1981, 6.75" x 9" x 1.75", Ceramic

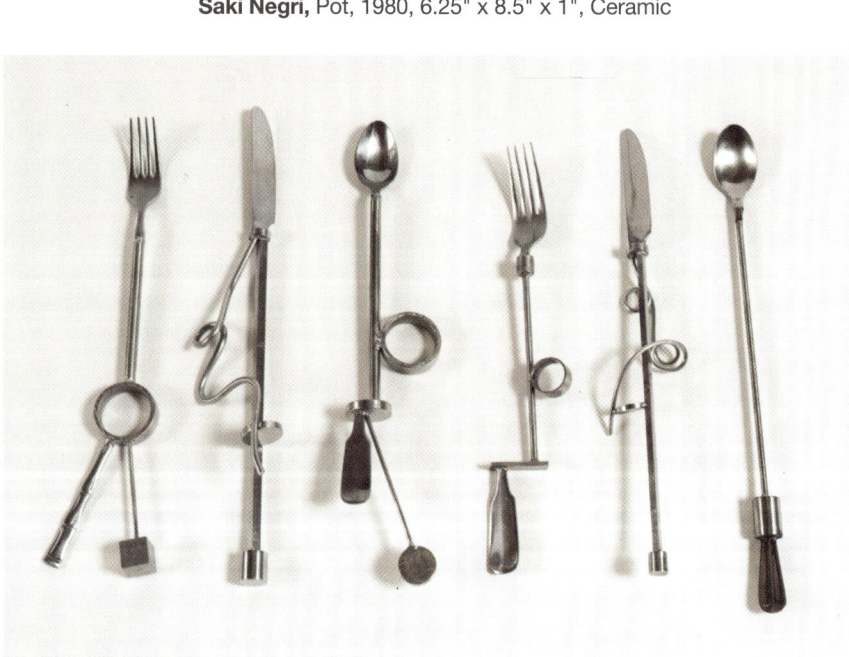

Signature Shire Flatware, 14" length maximum, Stainless Steel

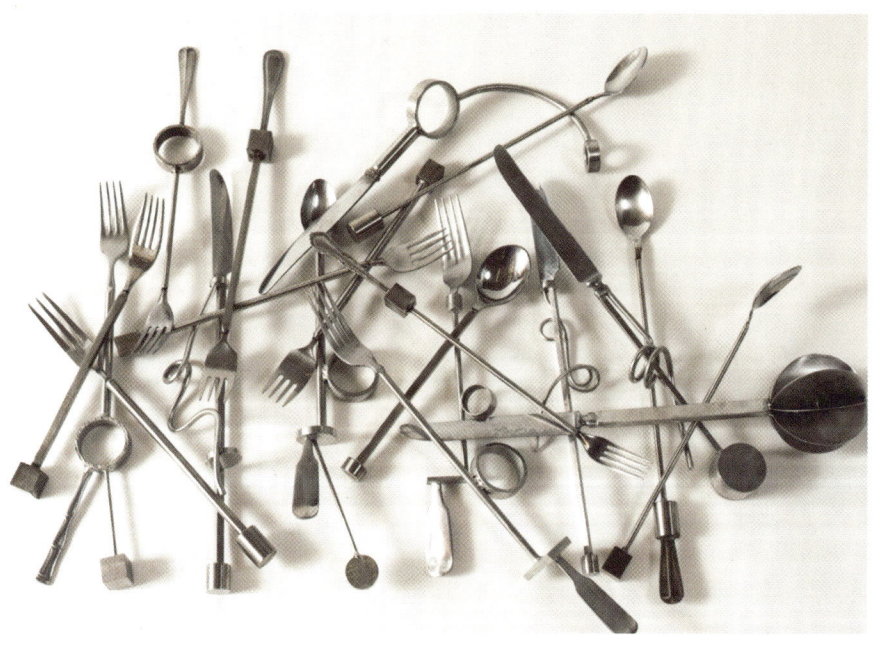

Signature Shire Flatware, 14" length maximum, Stainless Steel

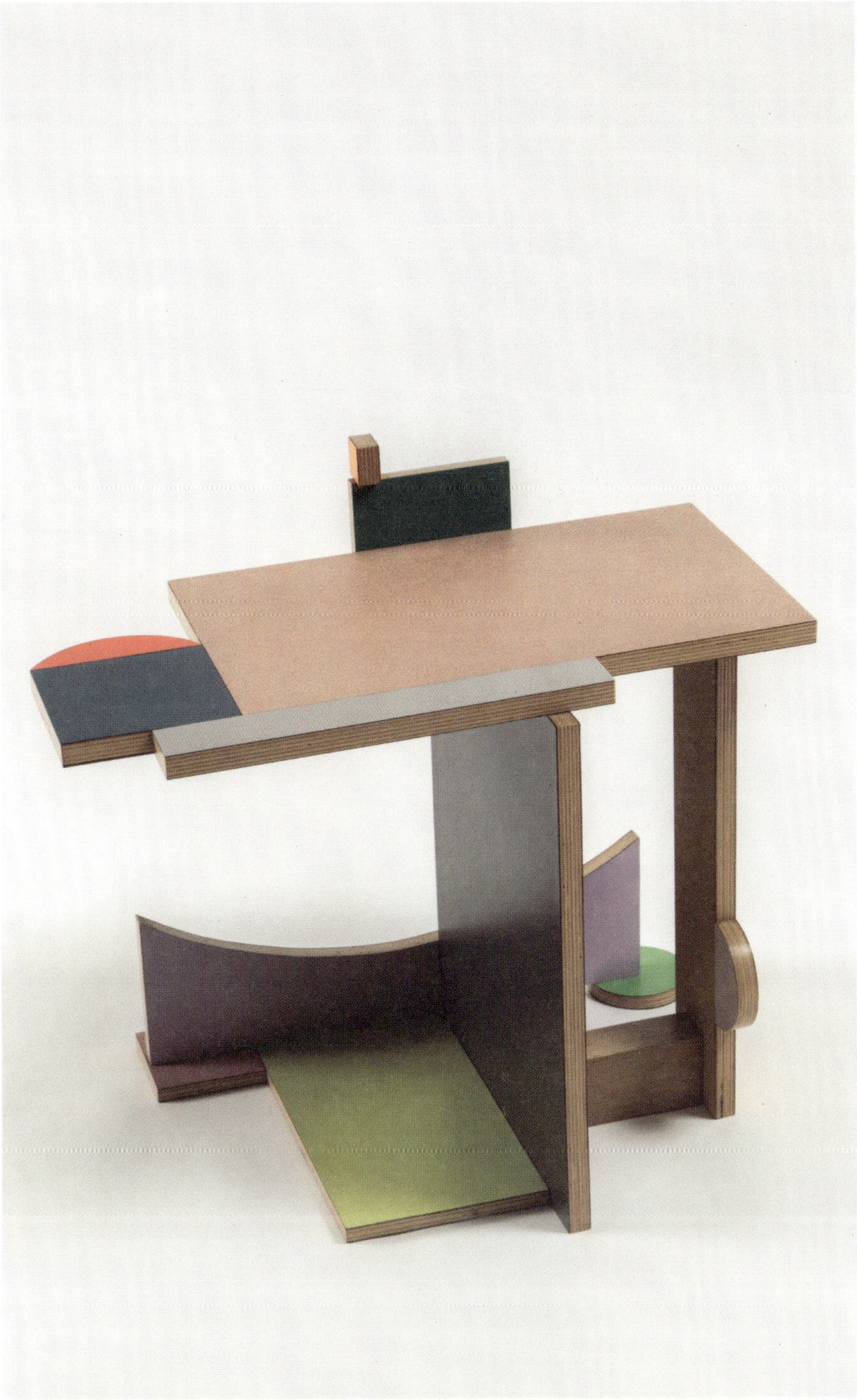

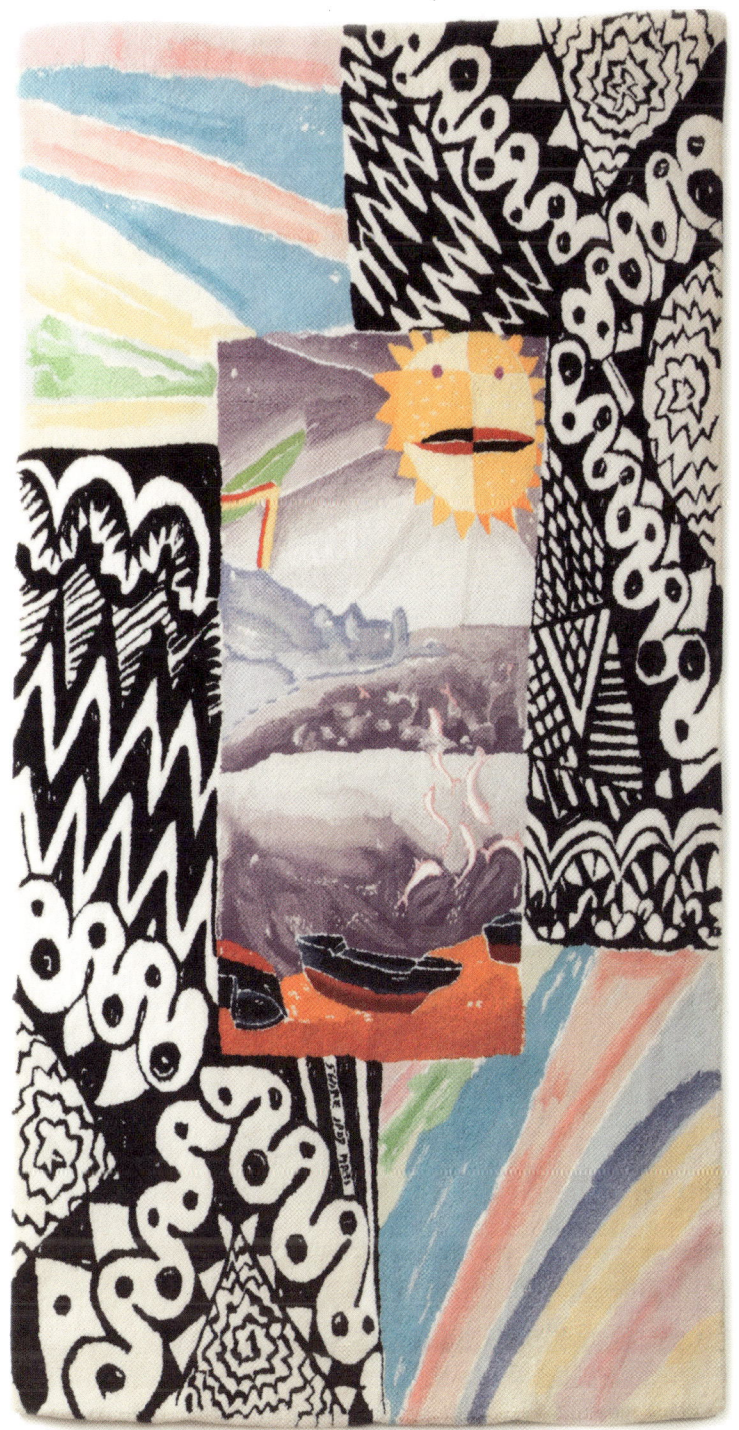

Rosa, Table, 1987, 20" x 26" x 14.5", Wood, laminate

French Hawaiian, Rug, c.1980, 87.5" x 63.5", Pure Wool, fabricated by TISCA, France

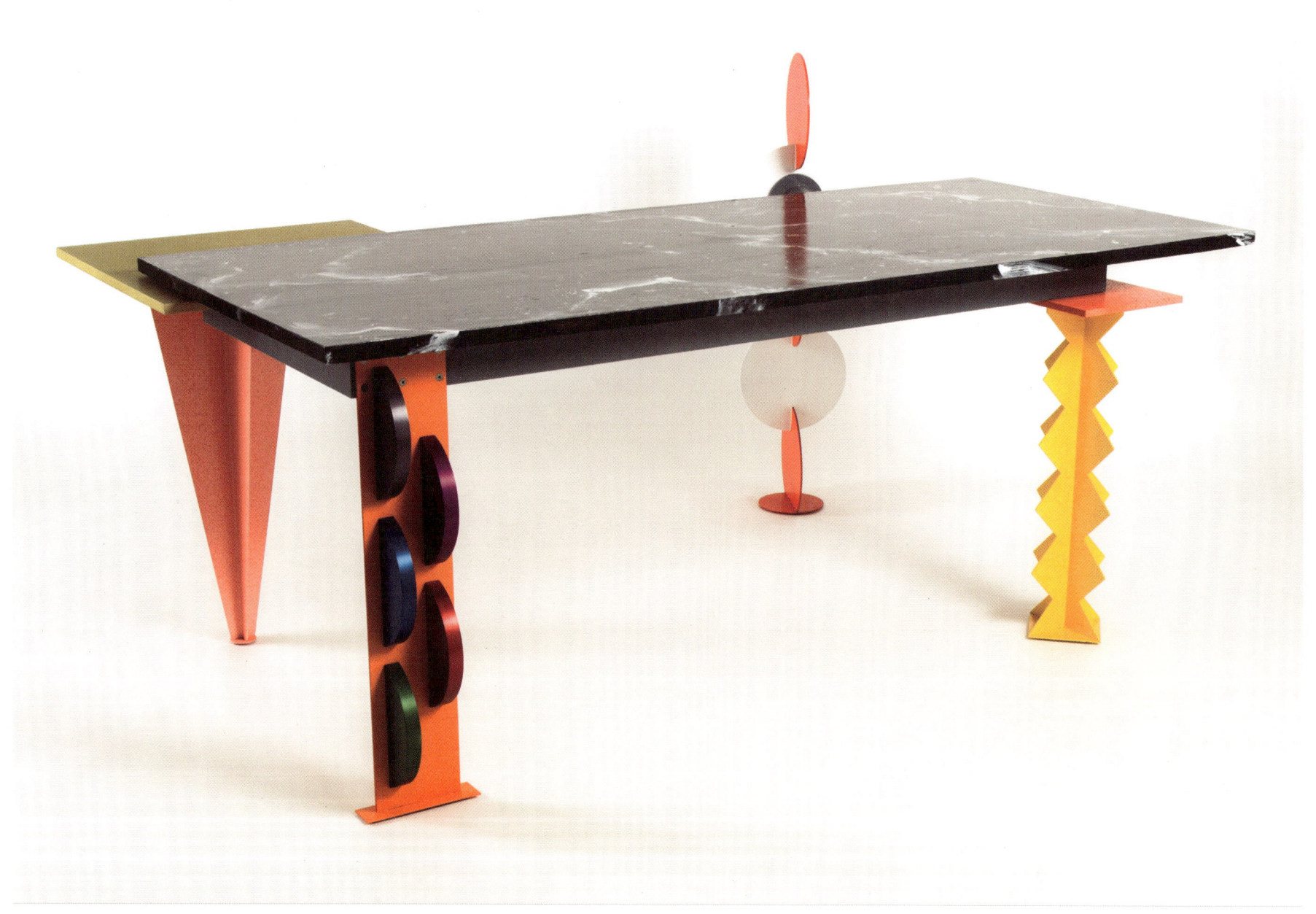

Harlequin, Table, 1982, 28.5" x 76" x 45", Steel, wood, enamel

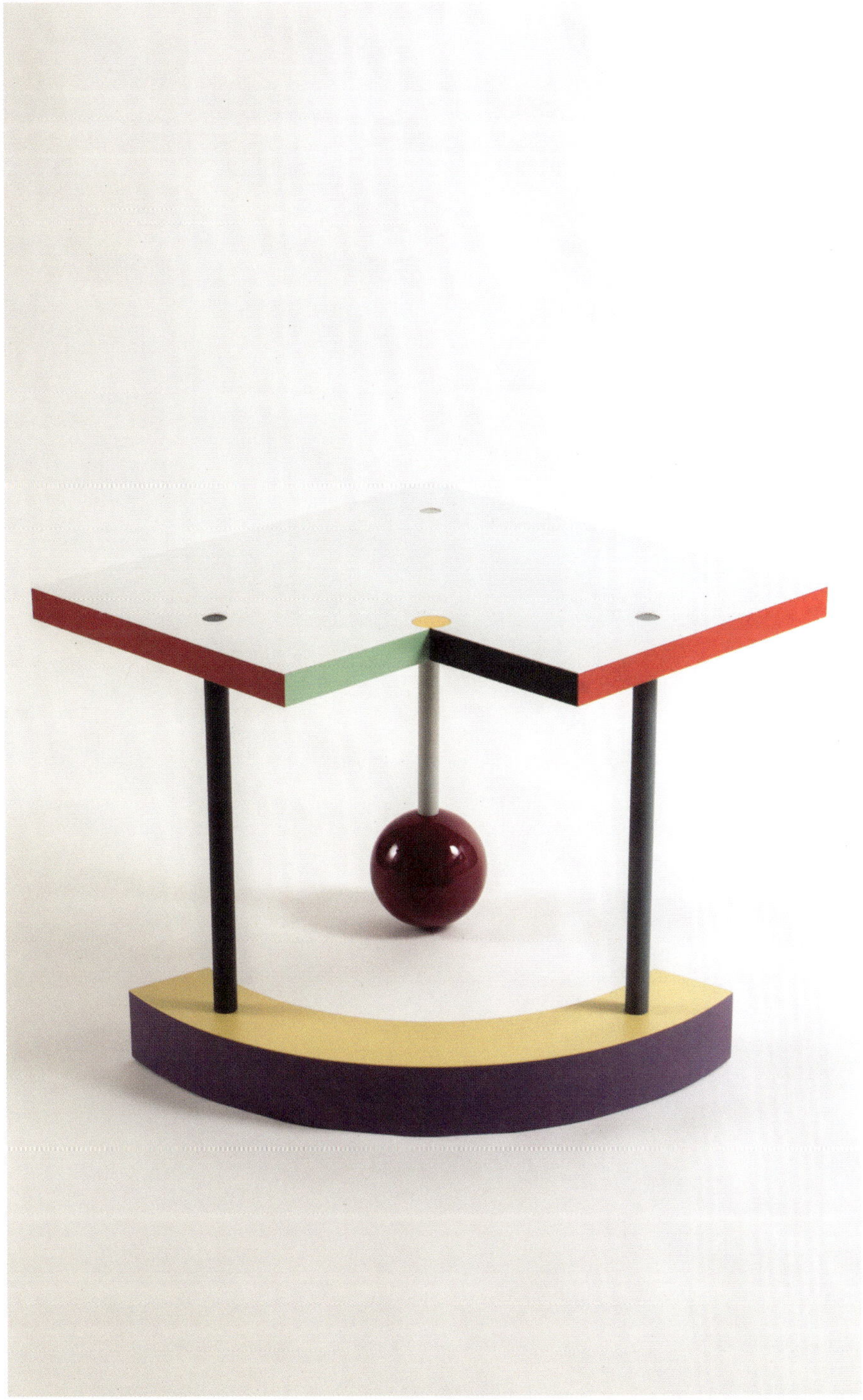

Hollywood, Table, MEMPHIS, 1983, 20" x 24" x 24", Wood, steel, laminate, enamel

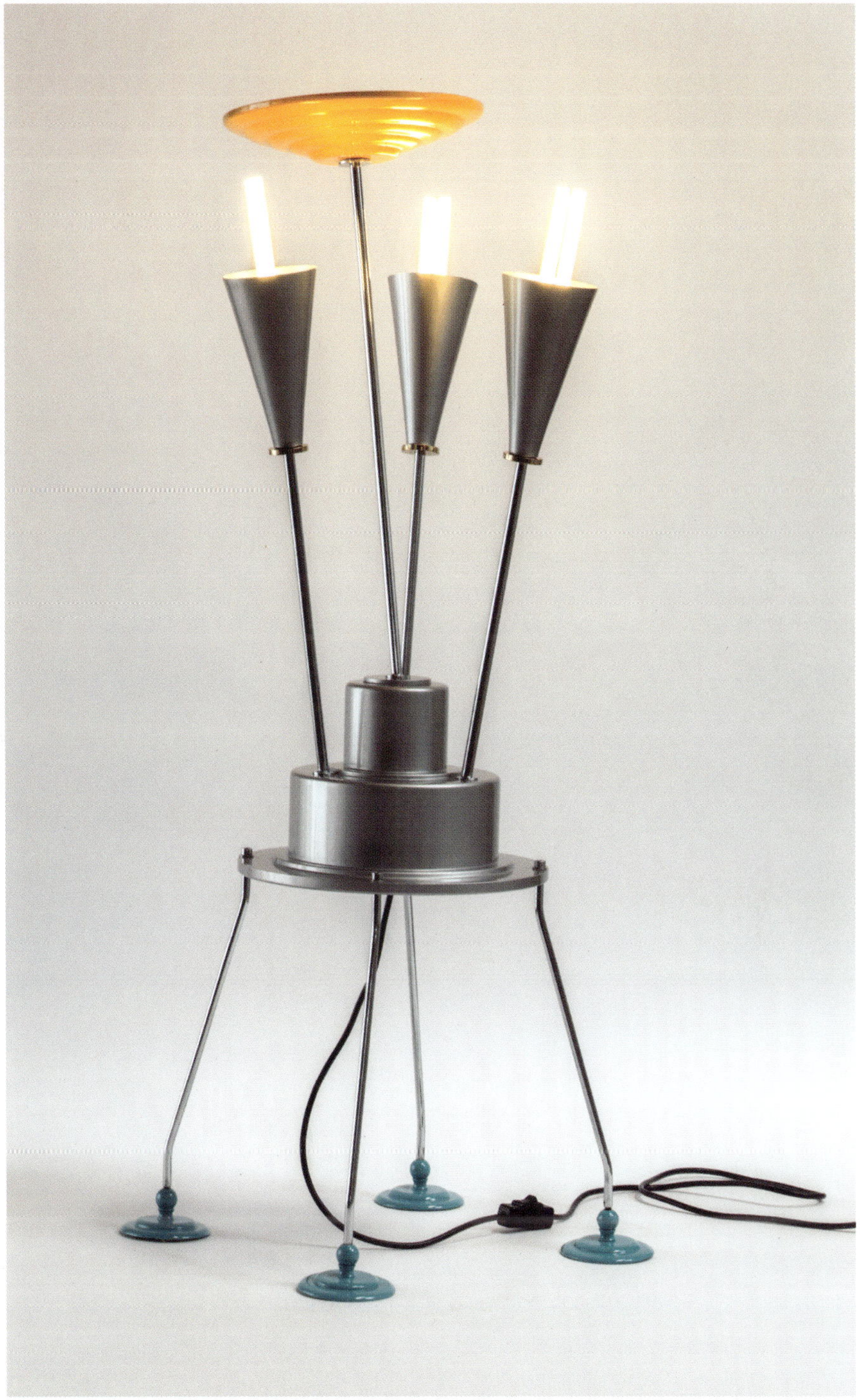

Cahuenga, Lamp, MEMPHIS, 1985, 39.75" x 18.5" x 19", Steel, chrome, enamel

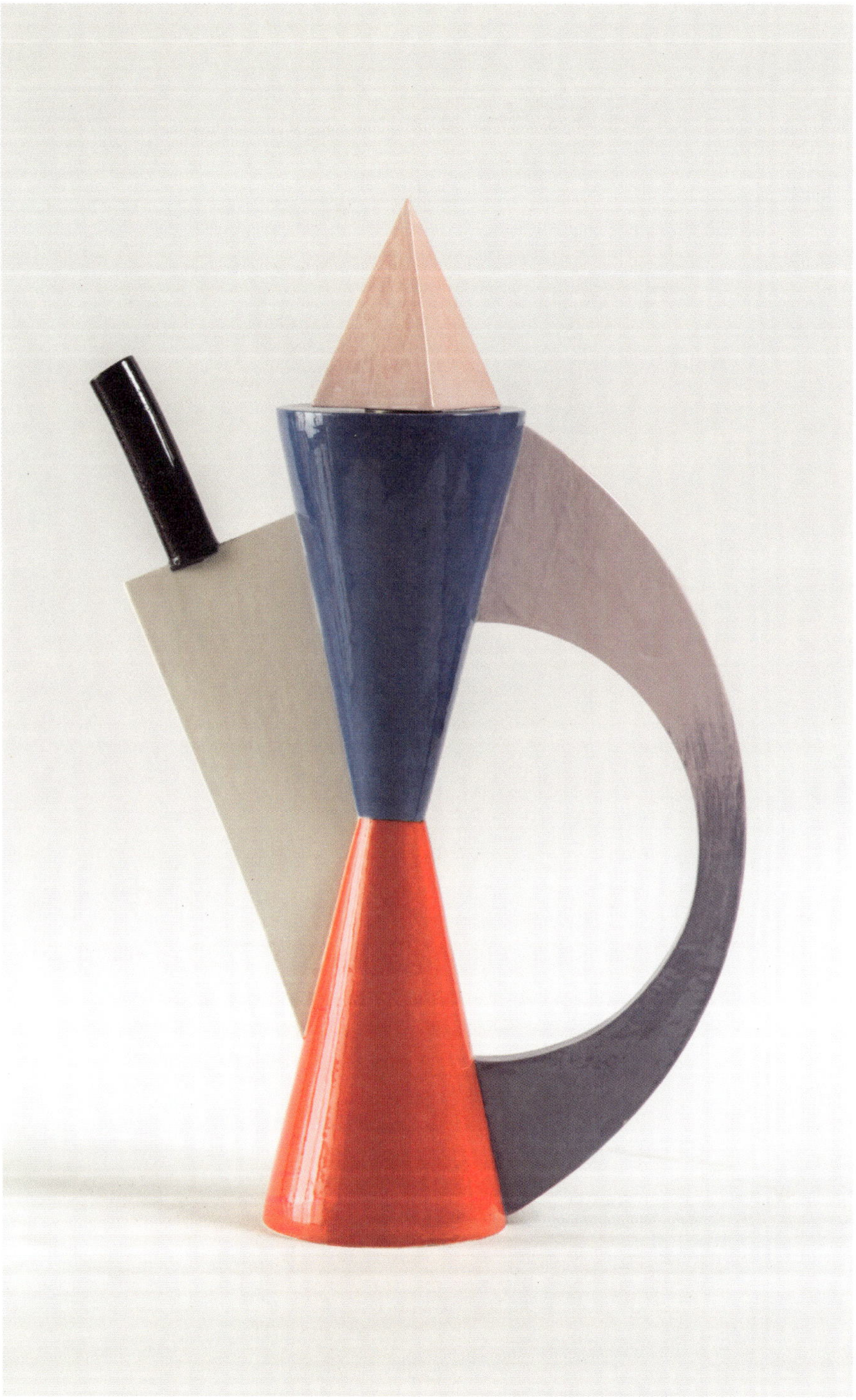

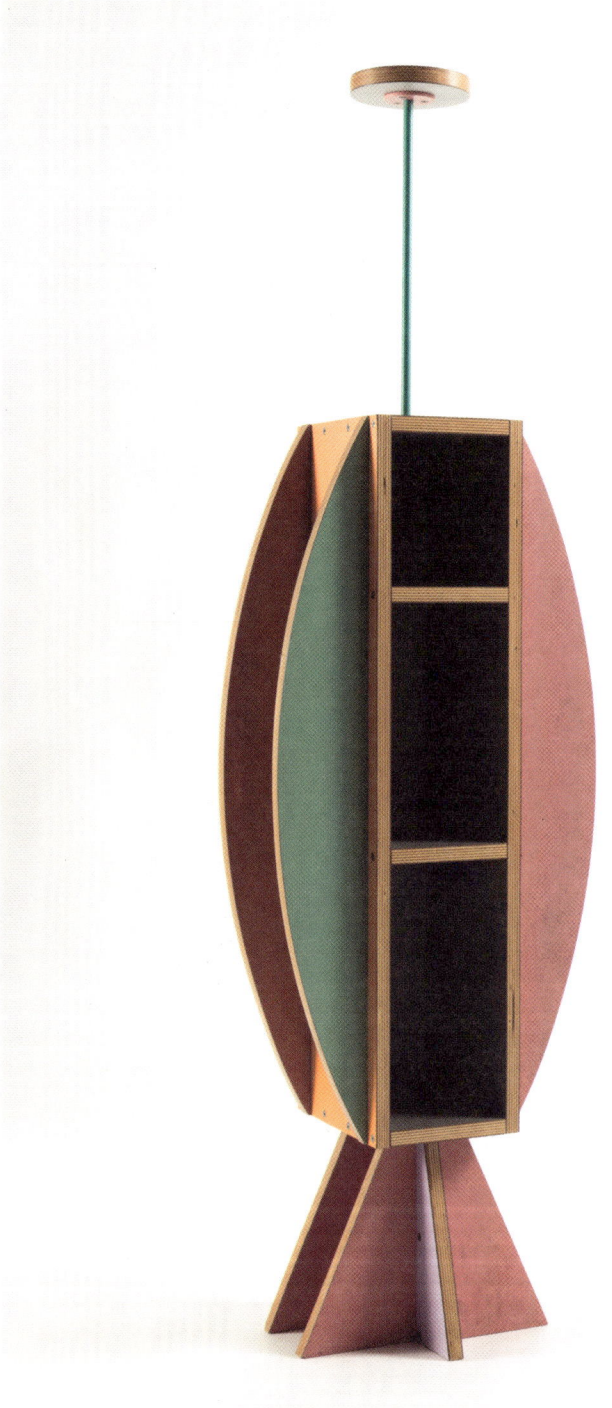

Hourglass, Teapot, 1984, 23" x 16" x 6", Ceramic

Rocket, Book Shelf, 1987, 58" x 10" x 18", Wood

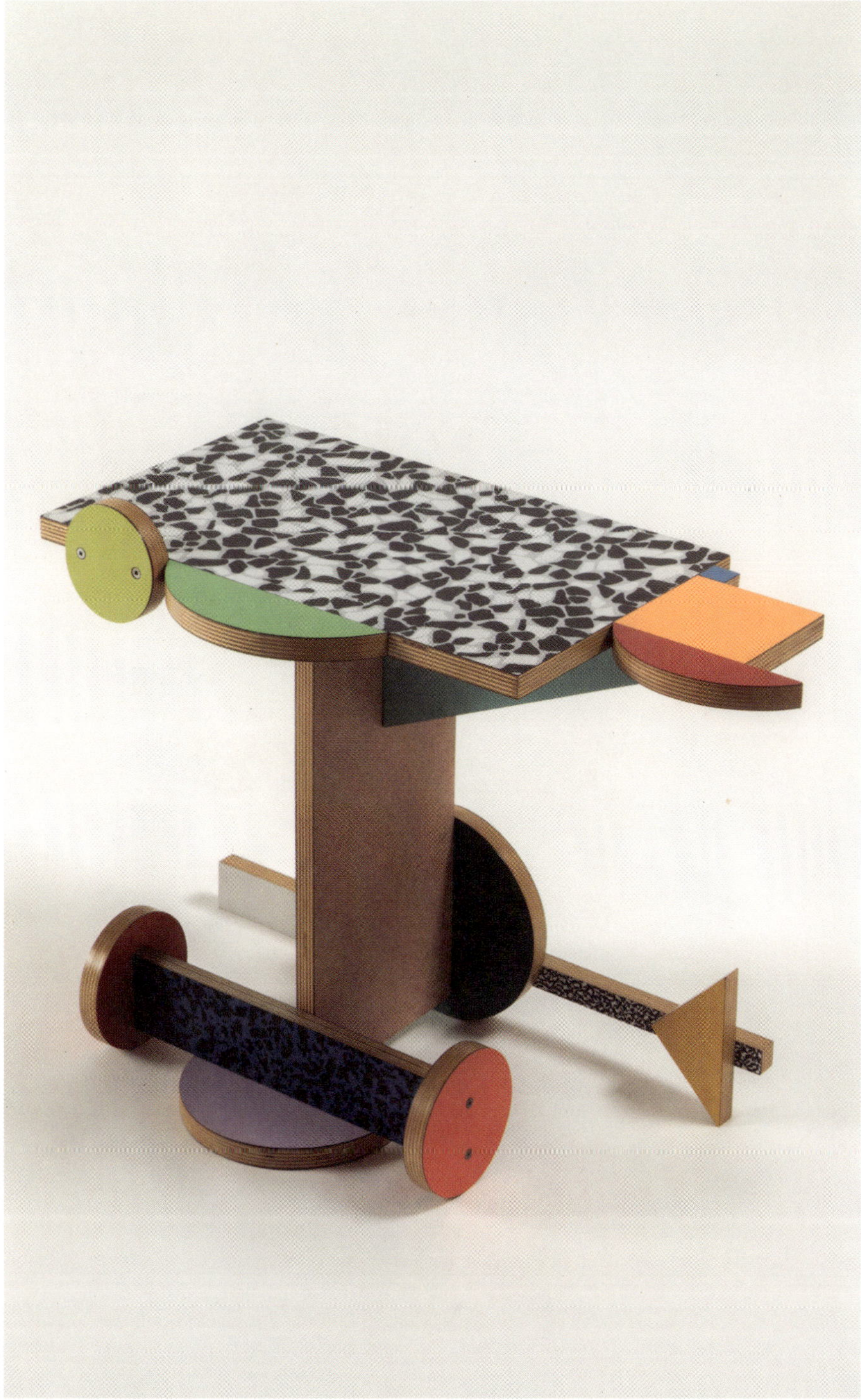

Negri & Bianchi, Table, 1987, 20" x 26.5" x 14.75", Wood, laminate

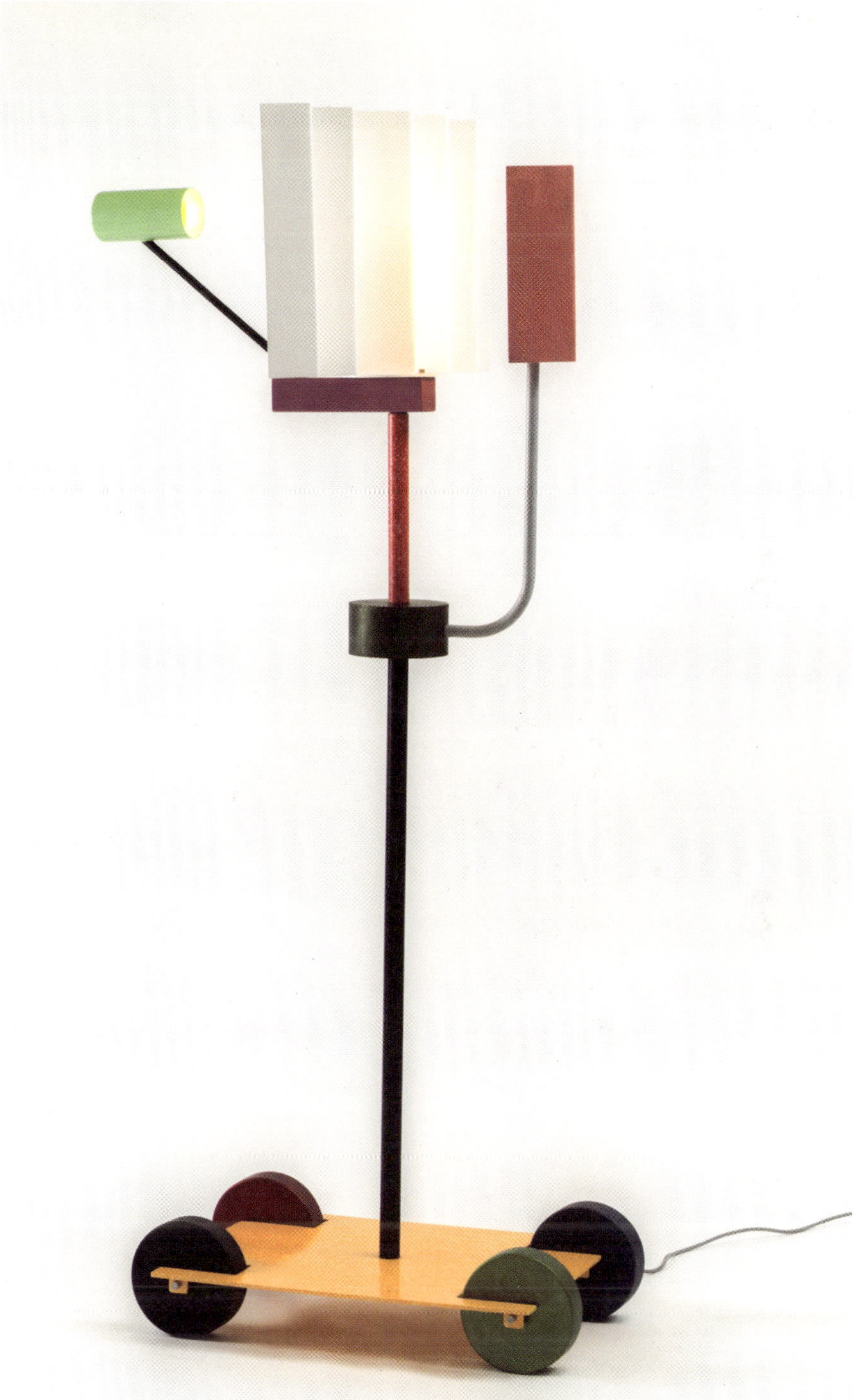

Bob-A-Re-Bob, Lamp, c.1990's, 71.5" x 40" x 27.5", Steel, chrome, enamel

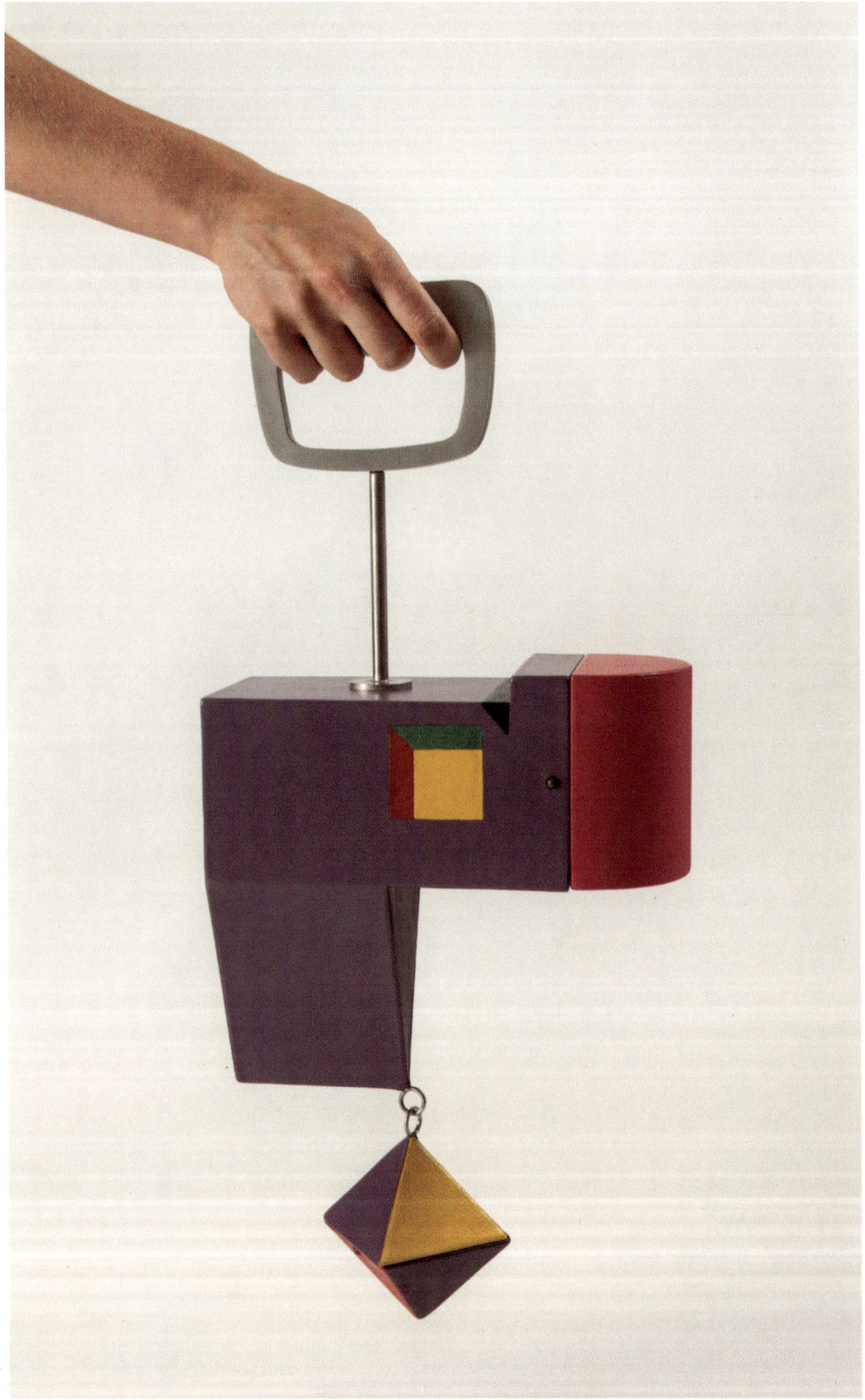

Evening Bag, Purse, Steel, leather, enamel

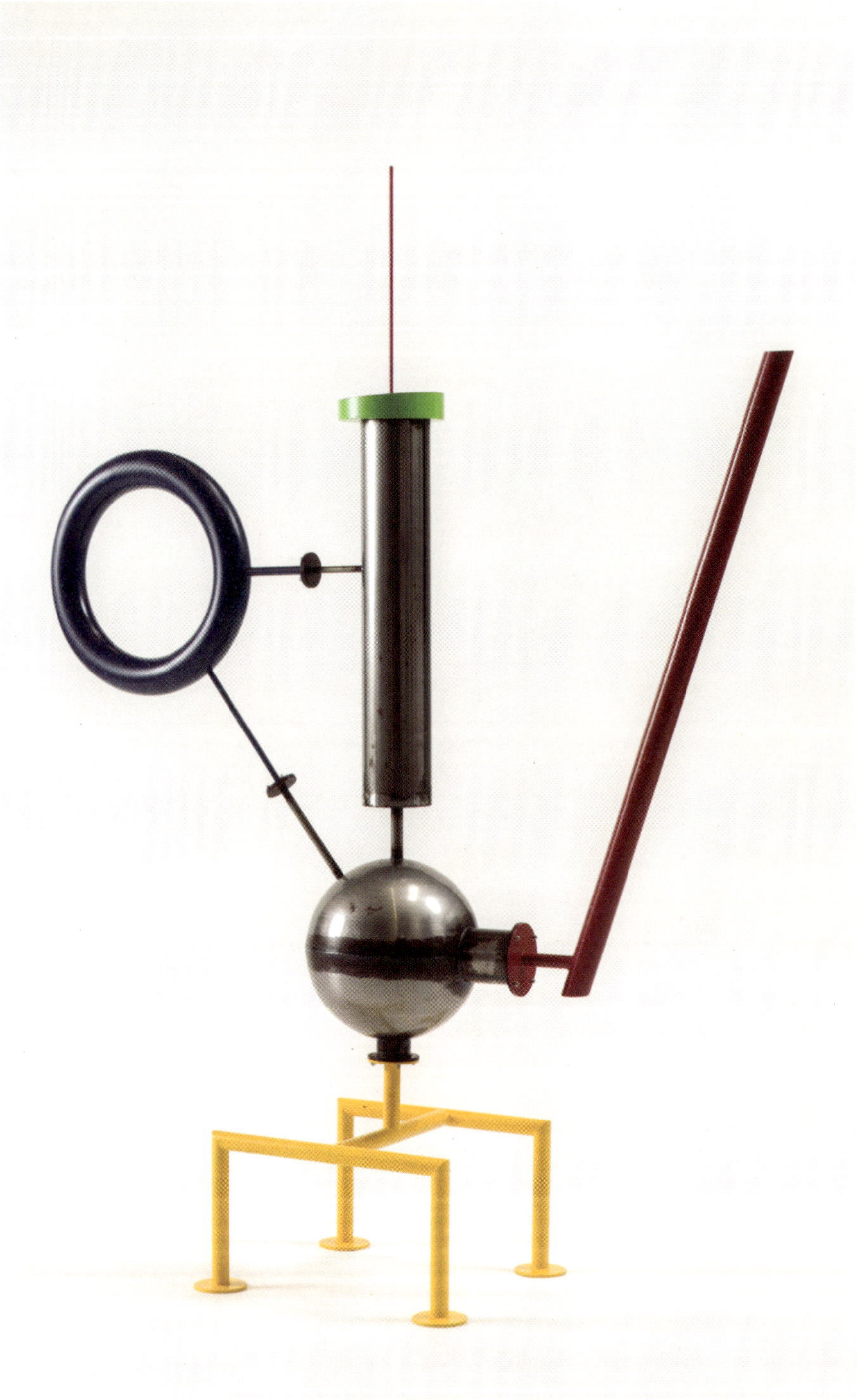

Giant Torso, Teapot, c.1990, 62" x 48" x 16", Steel

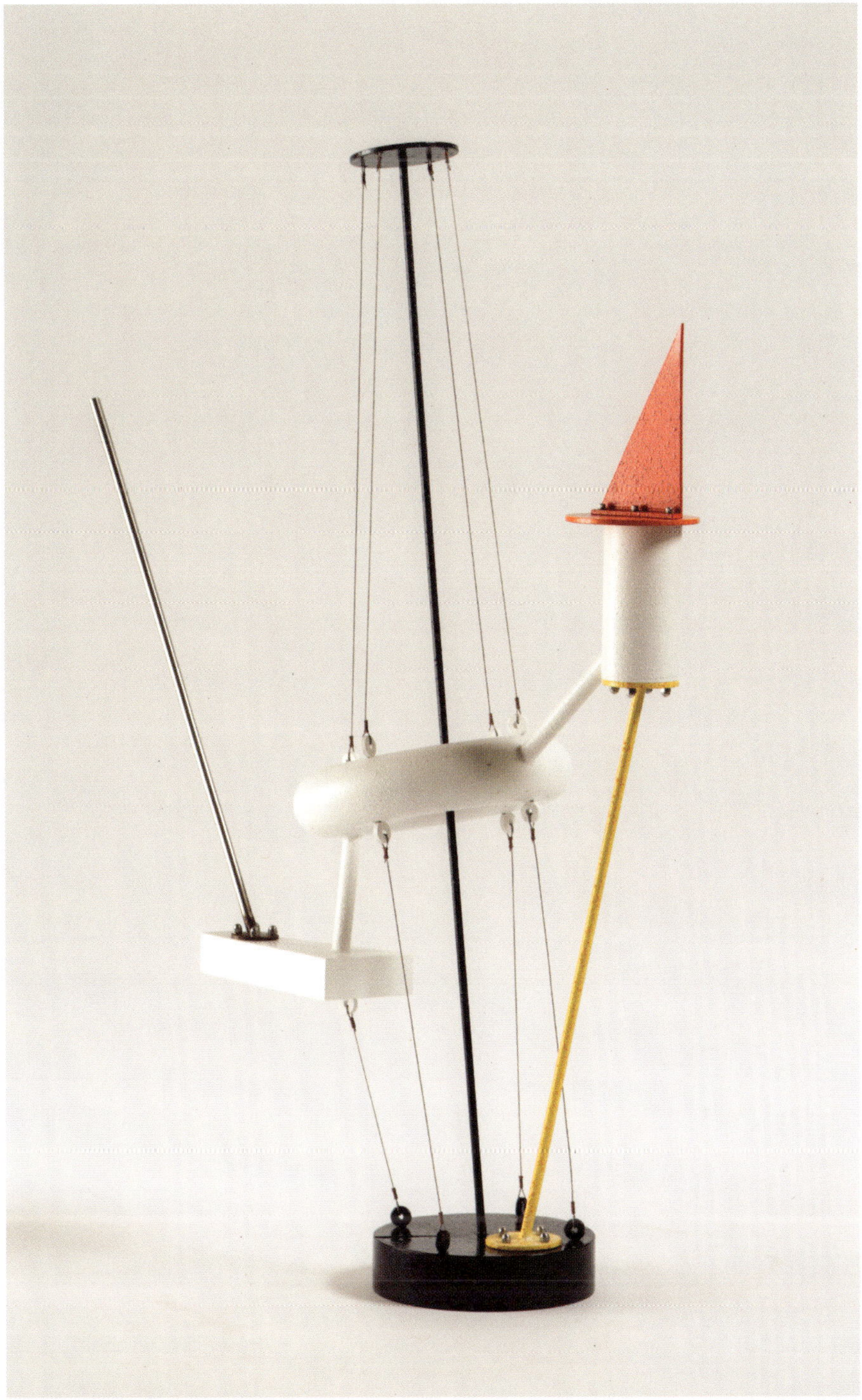

Micro Malevich Station, Teapot, c.1990, 30.5" x 23" x 8", Steel, chrome, enamel

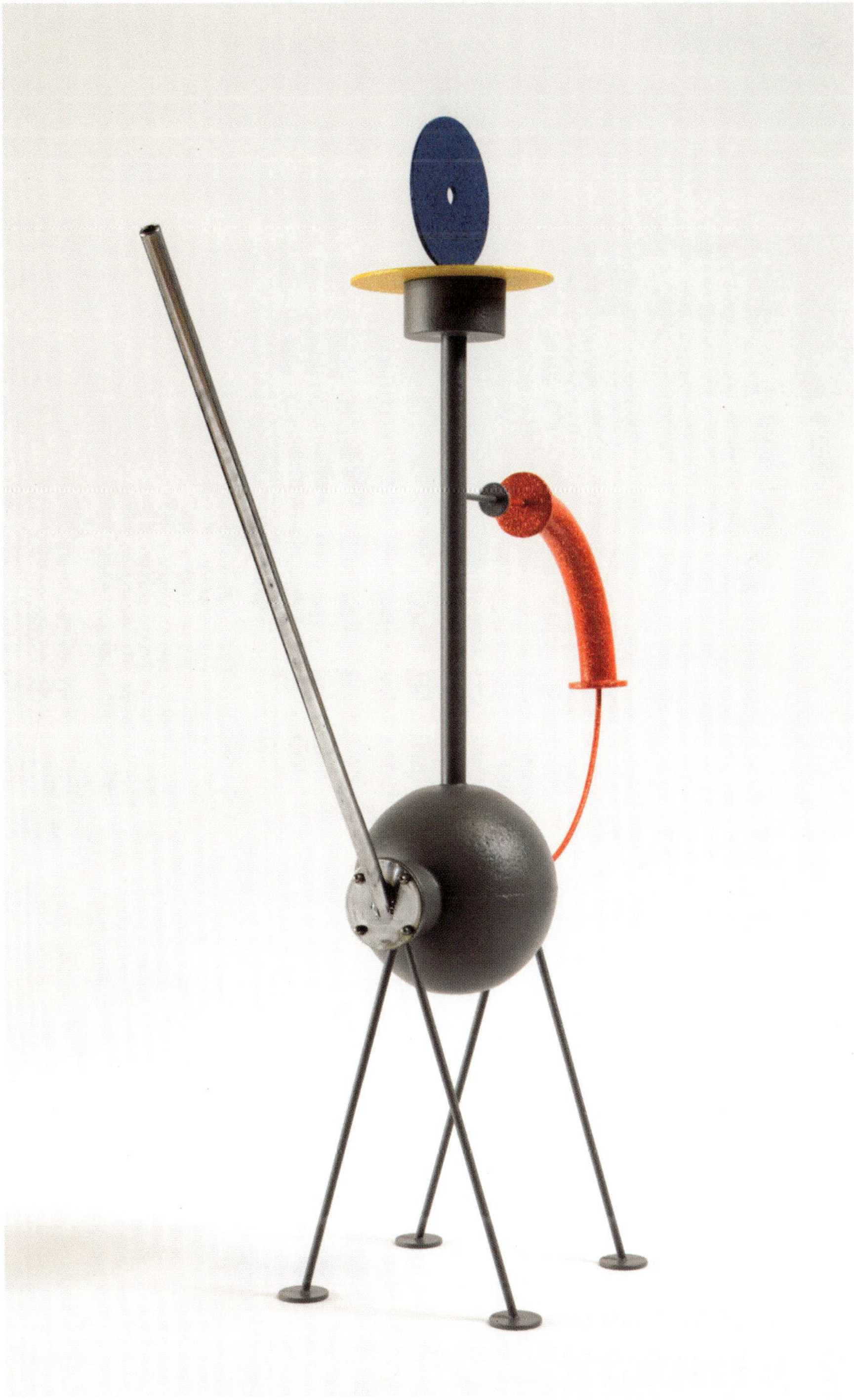

Torso Grigio, Teapot, c.1990, 25.5" x 24" x 8", Steel, chrome, enamel

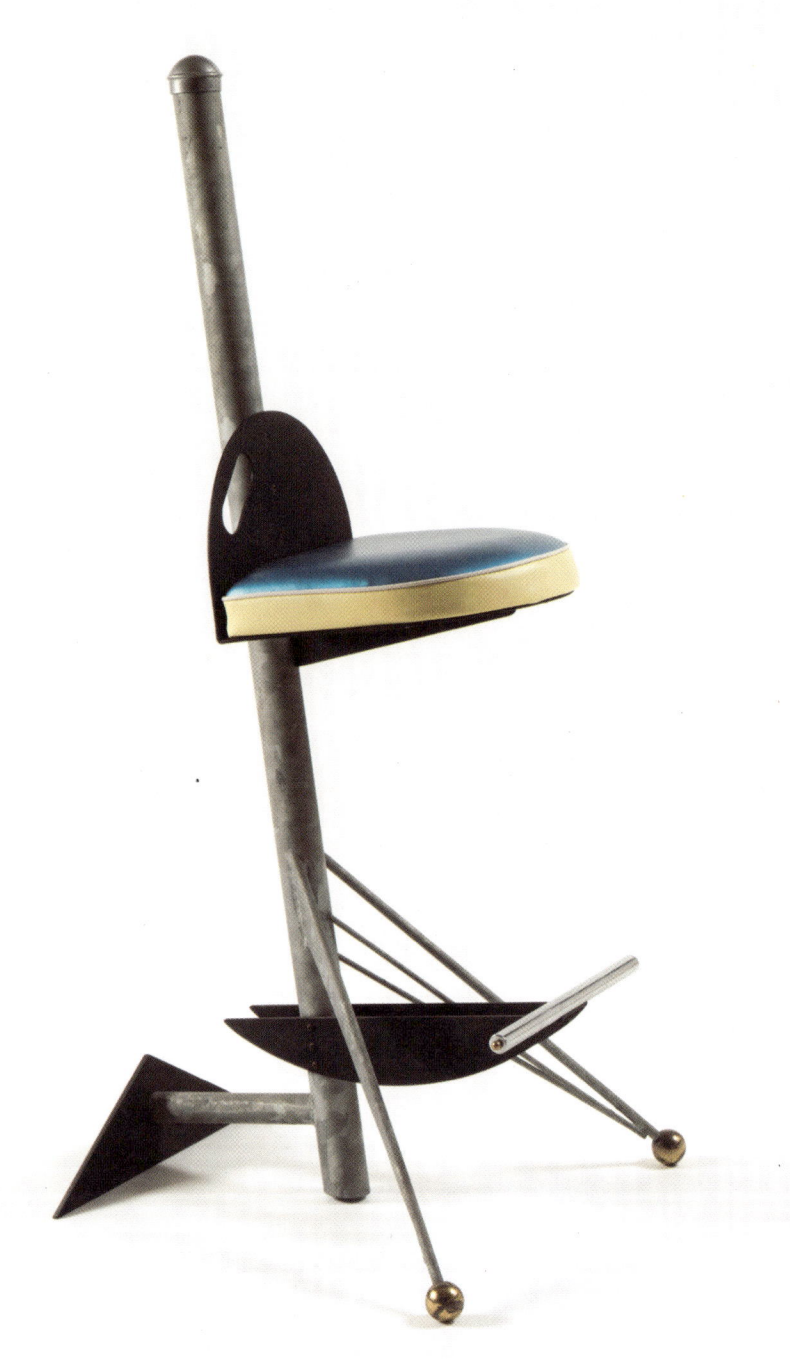

Tripod, Chair, c.1990's, 45.5" x 21" x 21.5", Galvanized steel, enamel, upholstery   **Handbag Wheelie,** Purse, Fabricated by MARTEL, 38.5" x 15" x 5", Steel, leather, enamel

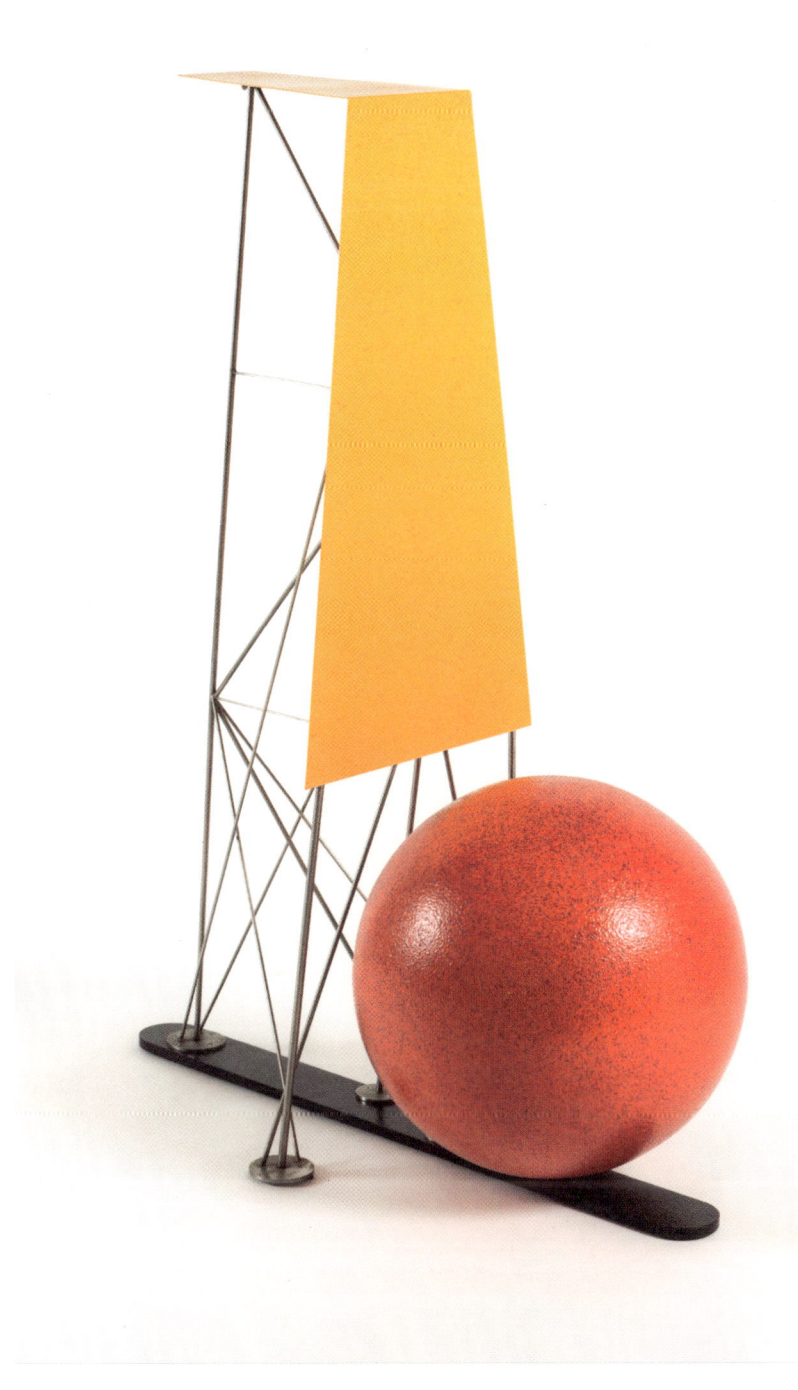

Oh My Cats, Chair, 2007, 48" x 18" x 39", Steel, chrome, enamel

Guy Noir, Chair, 2007, 41.75" x 24.25" x 16", Steel, enamel

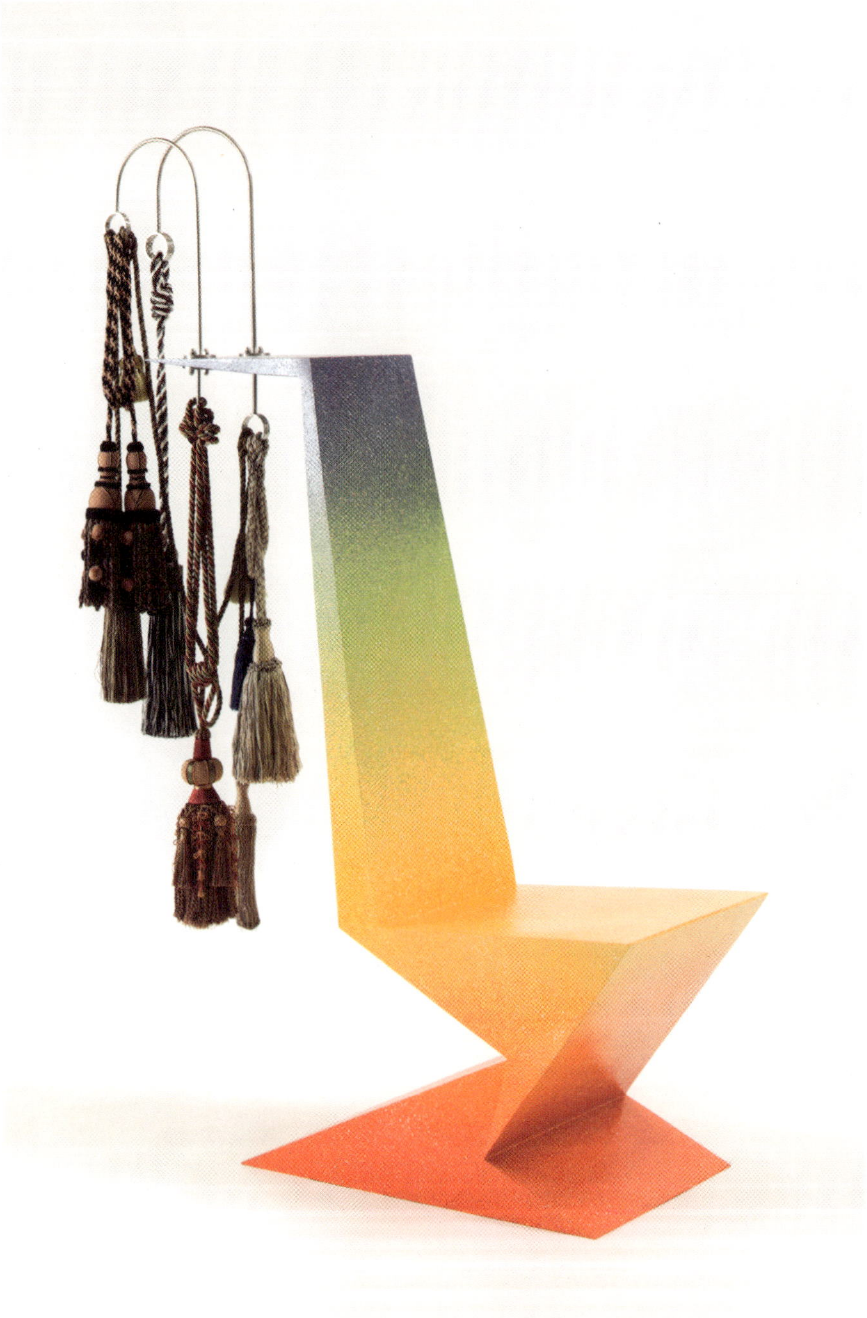

Right Weld, Chair, 2007, 63" x 43" x 16", Steel, enamel, tassels

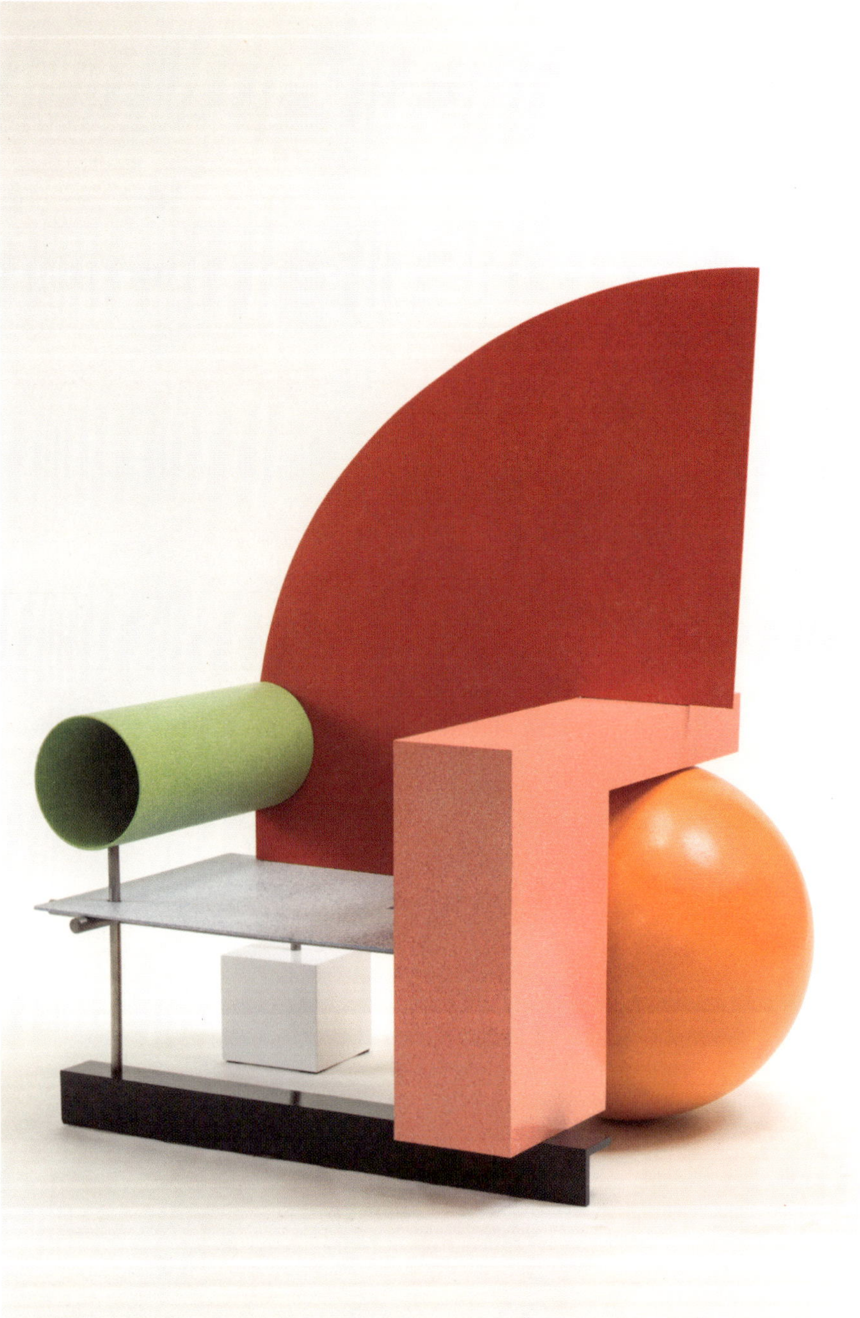

Belle Aire, Chair, 2010, 56" x 40" x 45.5", Steel, enamel

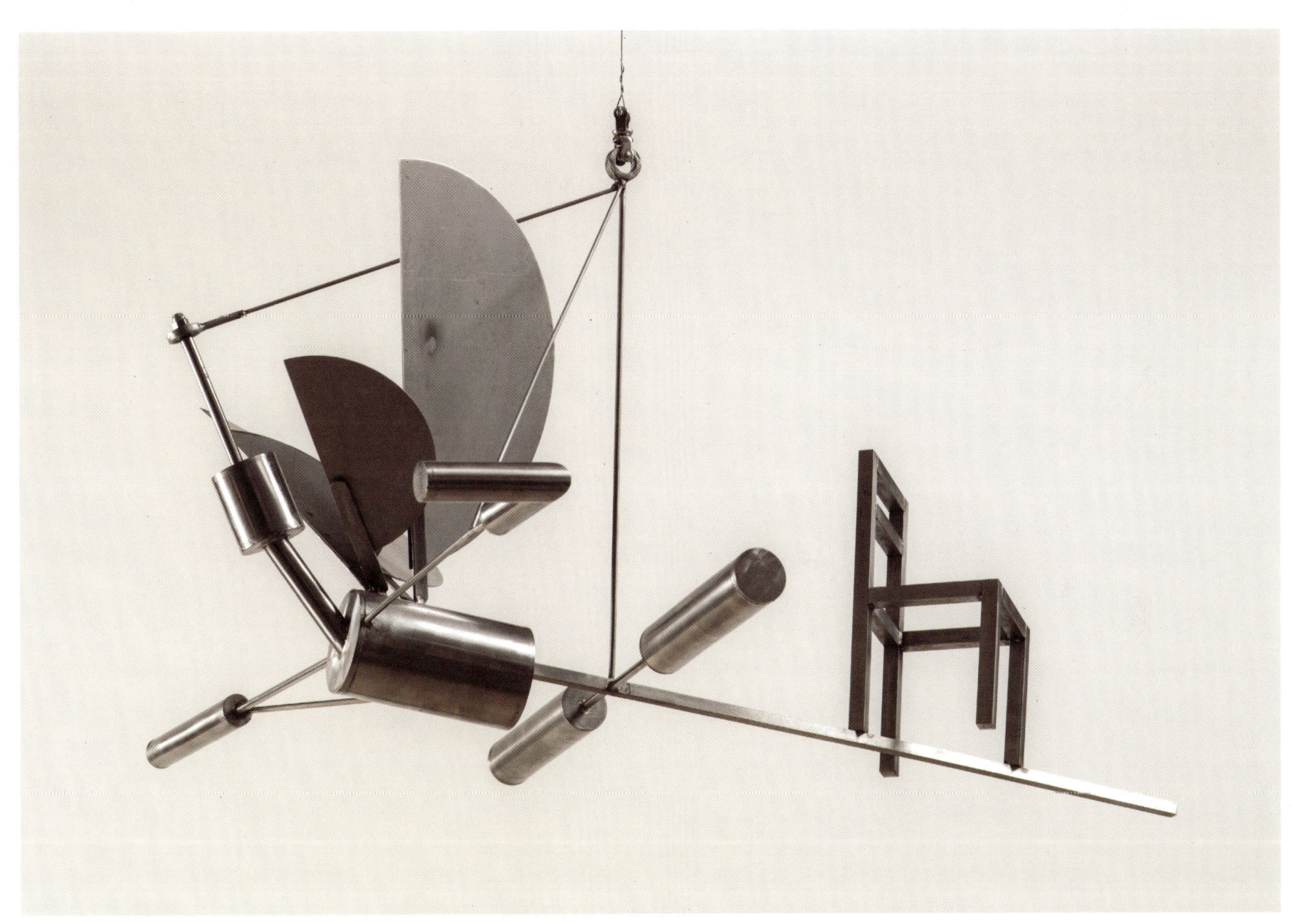

Flying Angel with Chair, Sculpture, c. 2000, 17.75" x 33" x 32", Stainless Steel

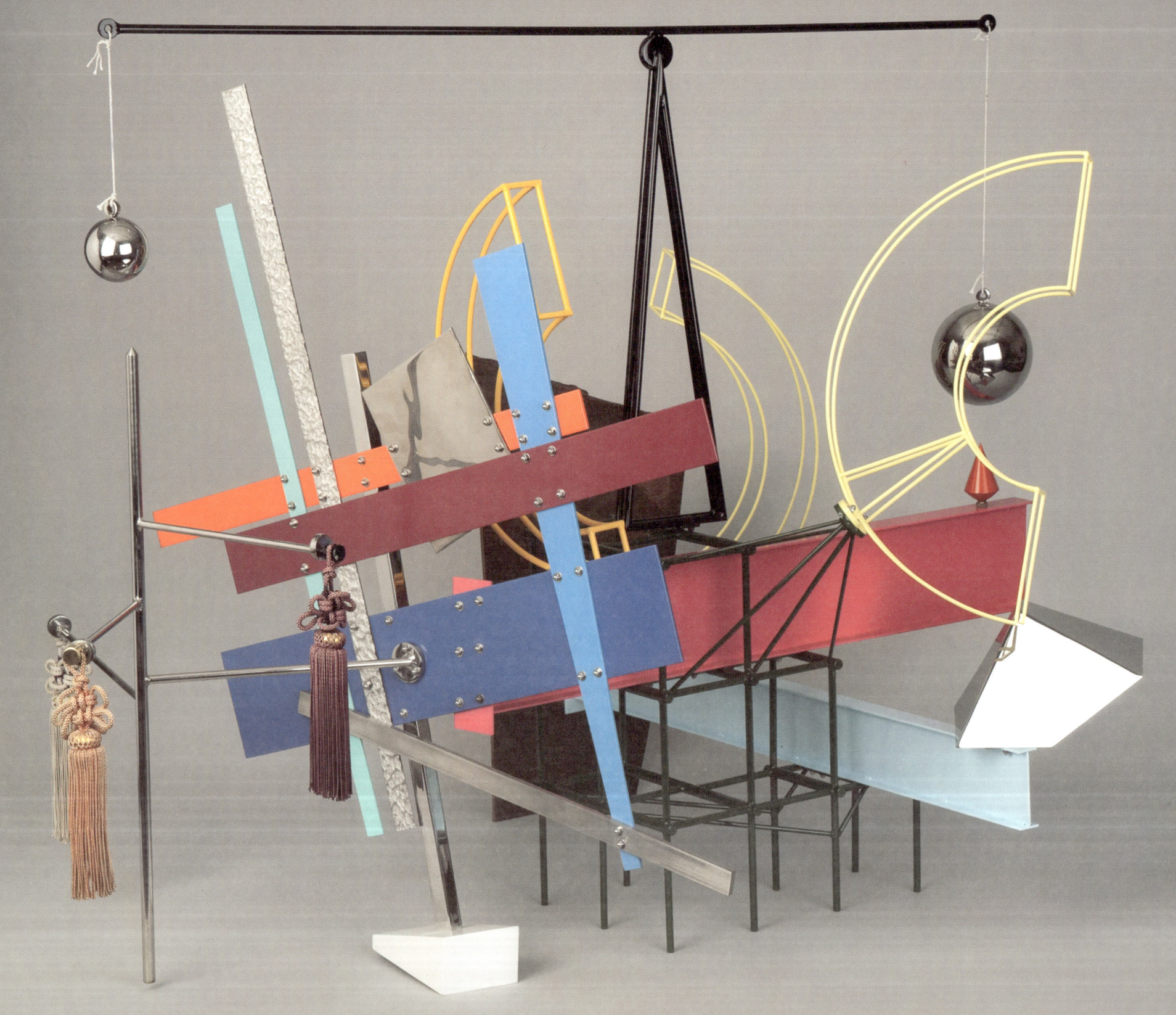

Glassell Gallery

Serious Fun:
Works by Peter Shire

The Palace at 4 am, HOKKAIDO, 1993, 30.5" x 19.5" x 37.5", Stainless Steel, enamel

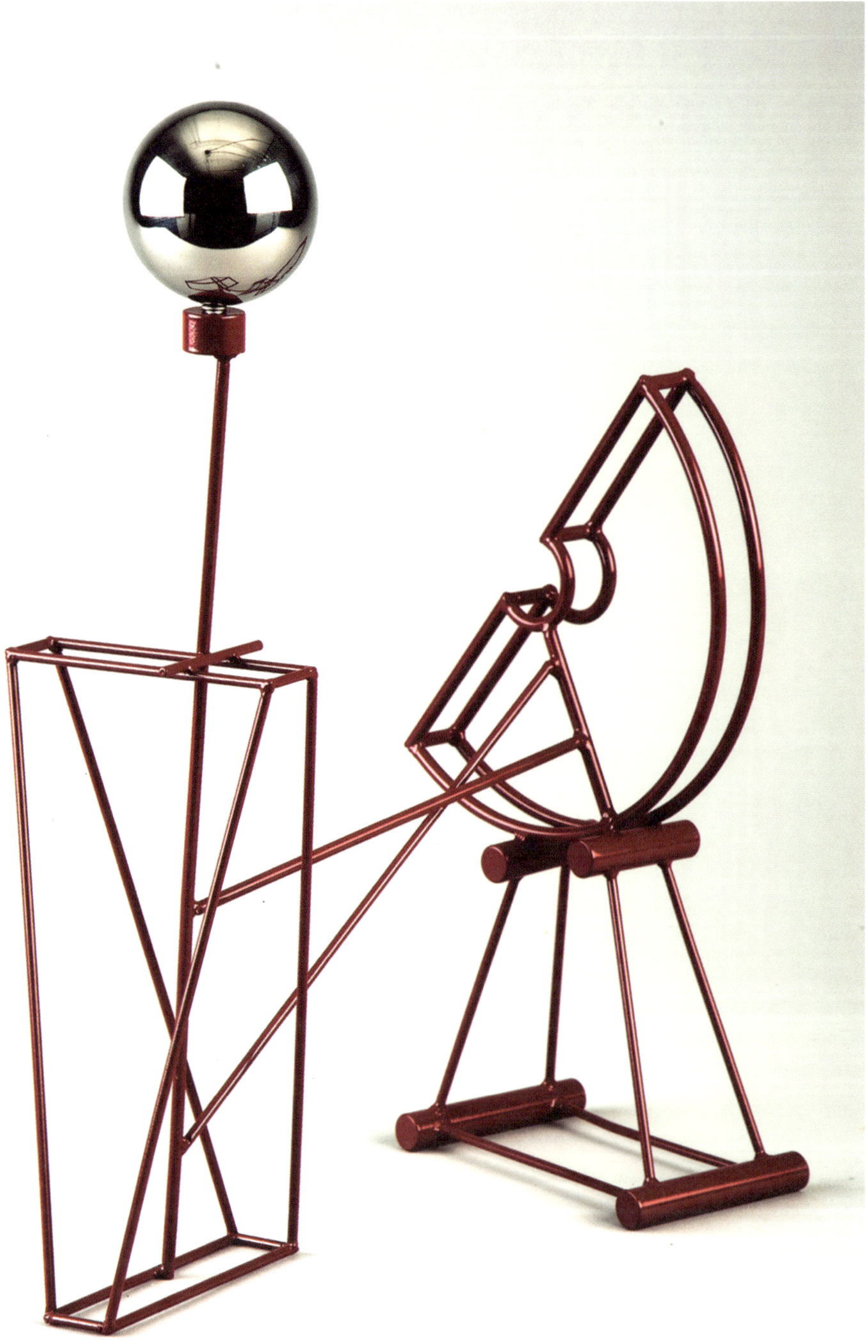

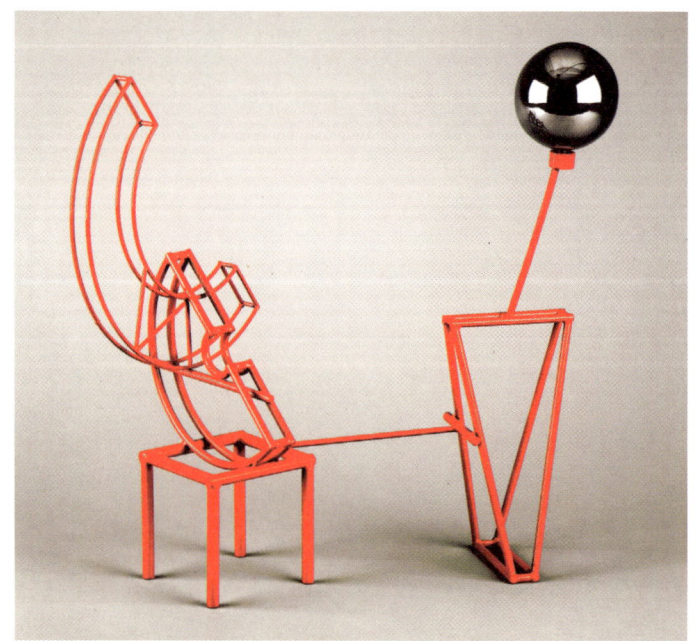

Gaijin, HOKKAIDO, 1993, 13.5" x 9" x 14", Stainless Steel, enamel

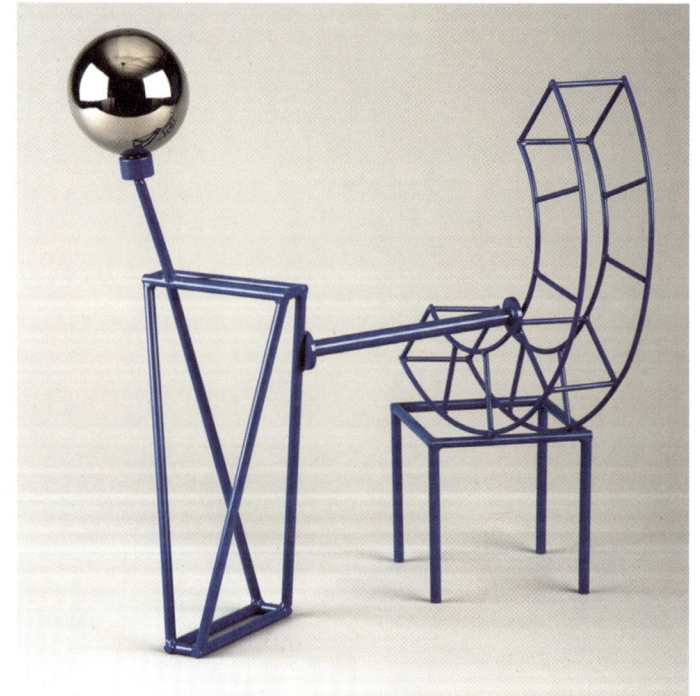

Maroon Crescent Yabanjin, HOKKAIDO, 1993, 14.5" x 6" x 30.25", Stainless Steel, enamel

Chimpira, HOKKAIDO, 1993 ,16.5" x 6" x 17", Stainless Steel, enamel

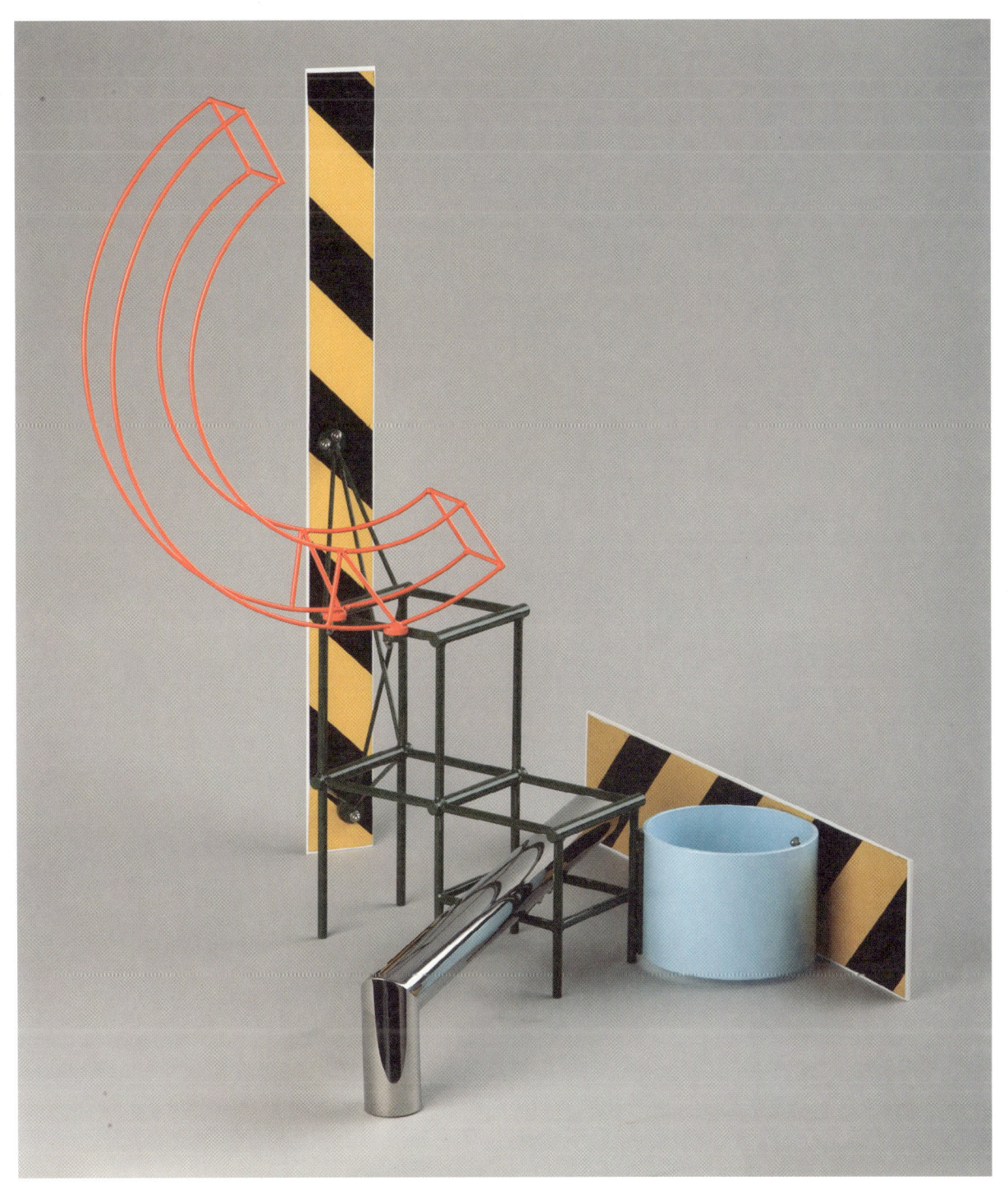

Genki, HOKKAIDO, 1993, 21.75" x 18" x 19", Stainless Steel, enamel

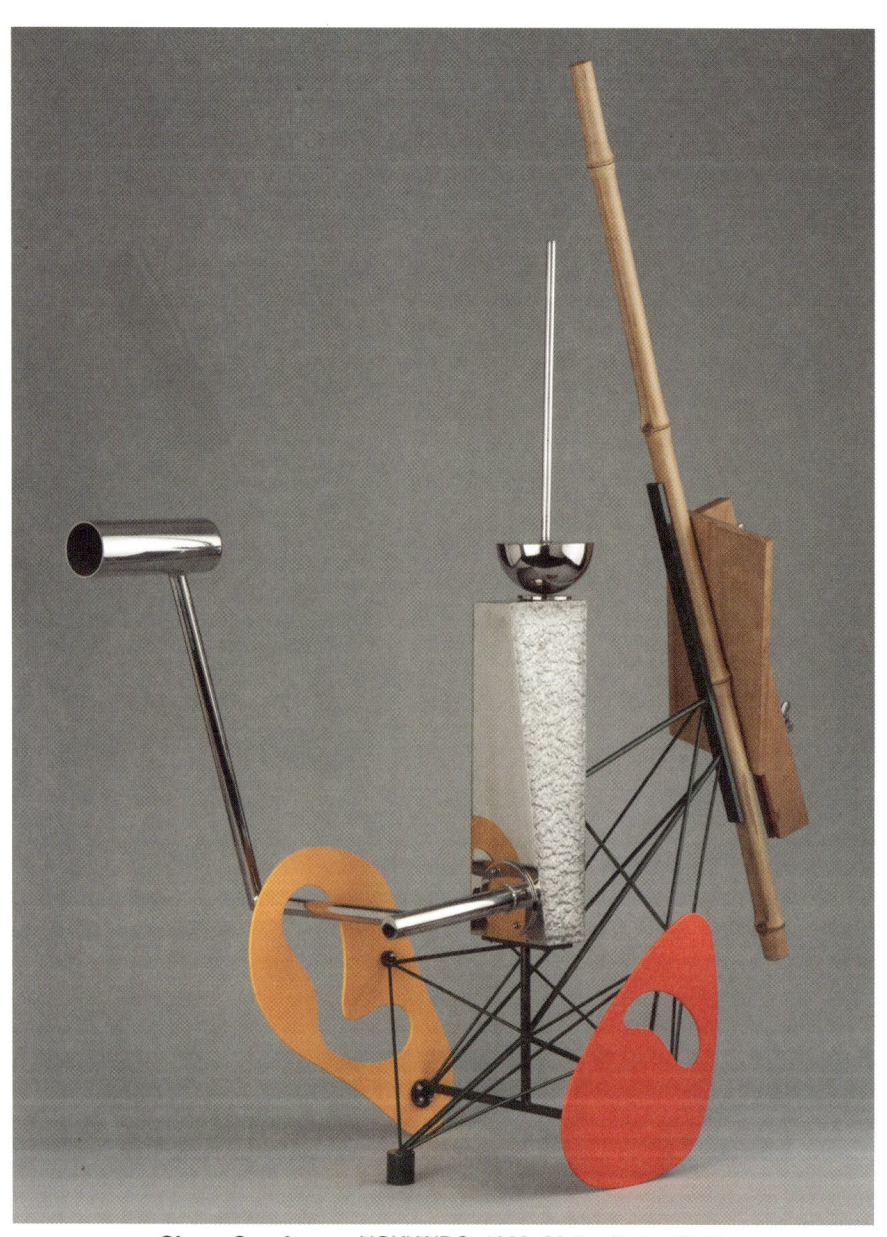

Ohayo Gozaimasu, HOKKAIDO, 1993, 38.5 x 15.5 x 26.5",
Stainless Steel, bamboo, enamel

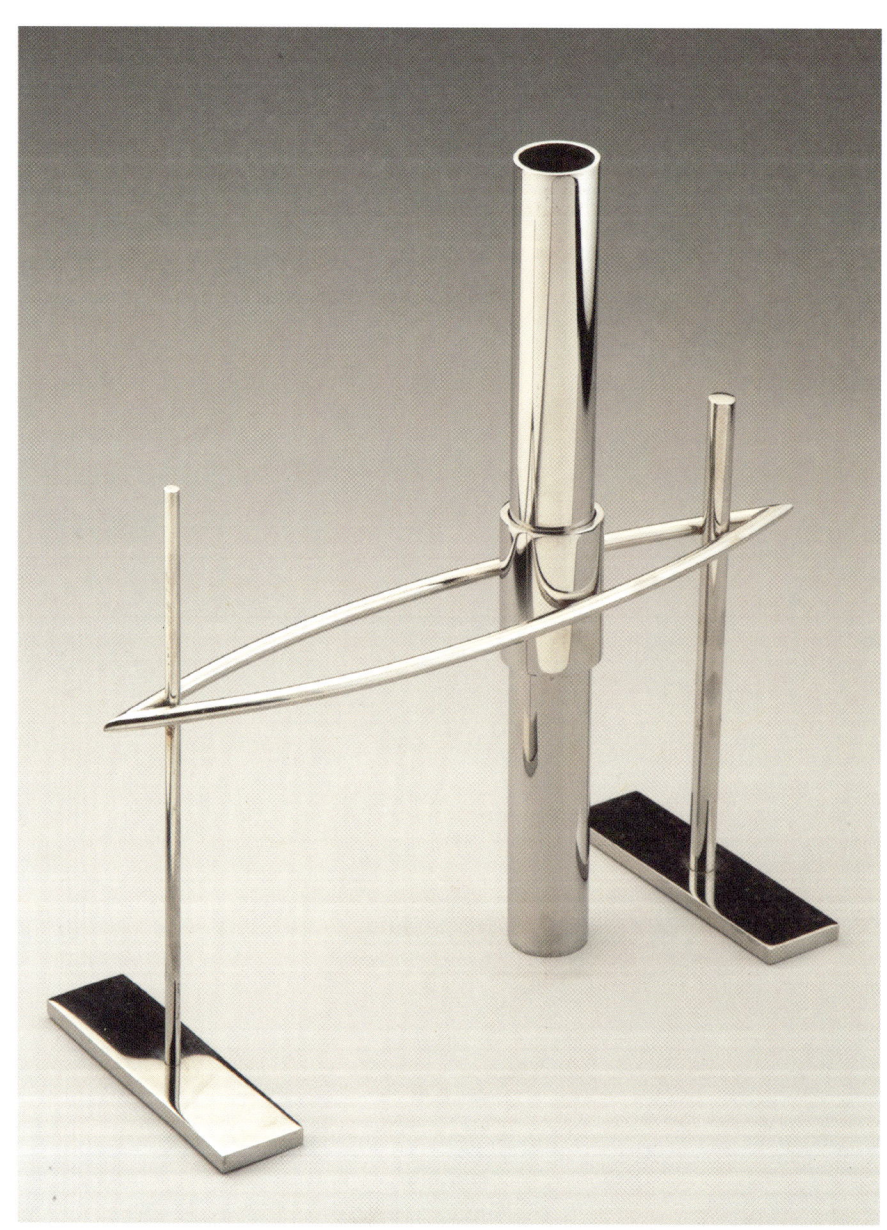

Two Lips on the Piano, HOKKAIDO, 1993, 10.75 x 4.5 x 10.5",
Stainless Steel

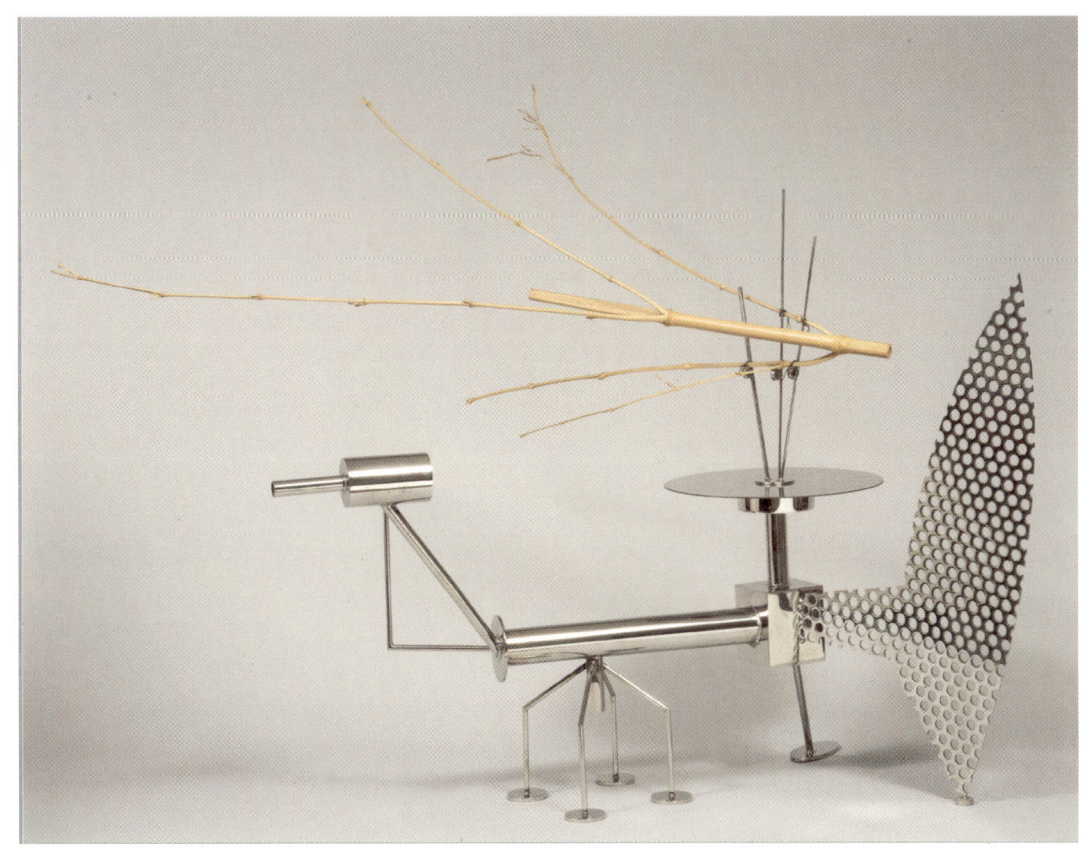

Blue Fin, HOKKAIDO, 1993, 18" x 13" x 45", Stainless Steel, bamboo

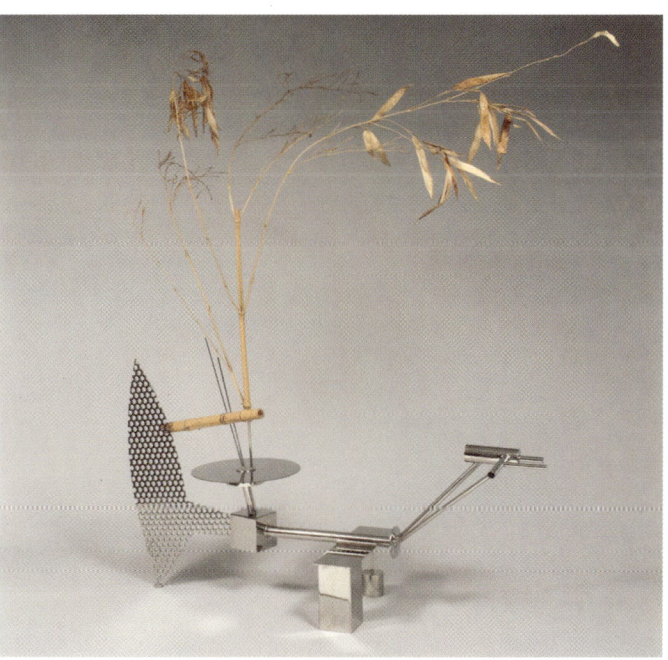

Kohada, HOKKAIDO, 1993, 19.5" x 22" x 44", Stainless Steel

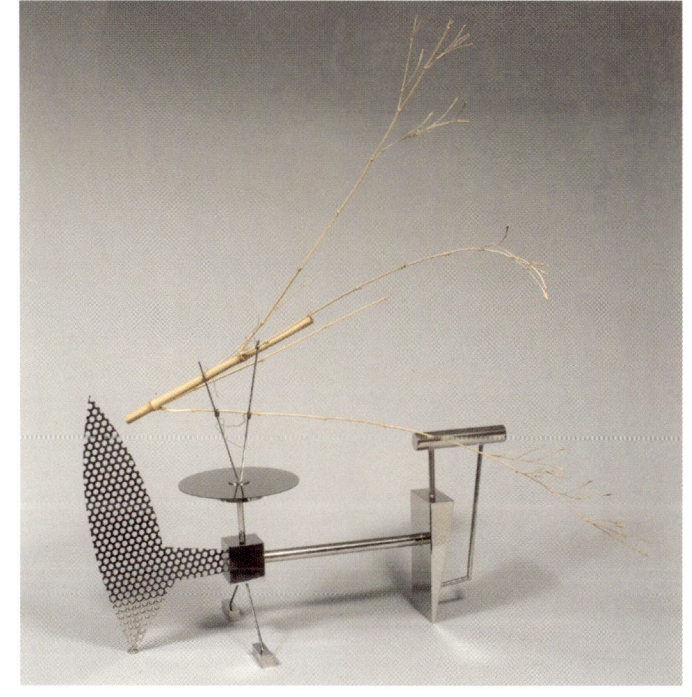

Maguro, HOKKAIDO, 1992, 48" x 12" x 45", Stainless Steel

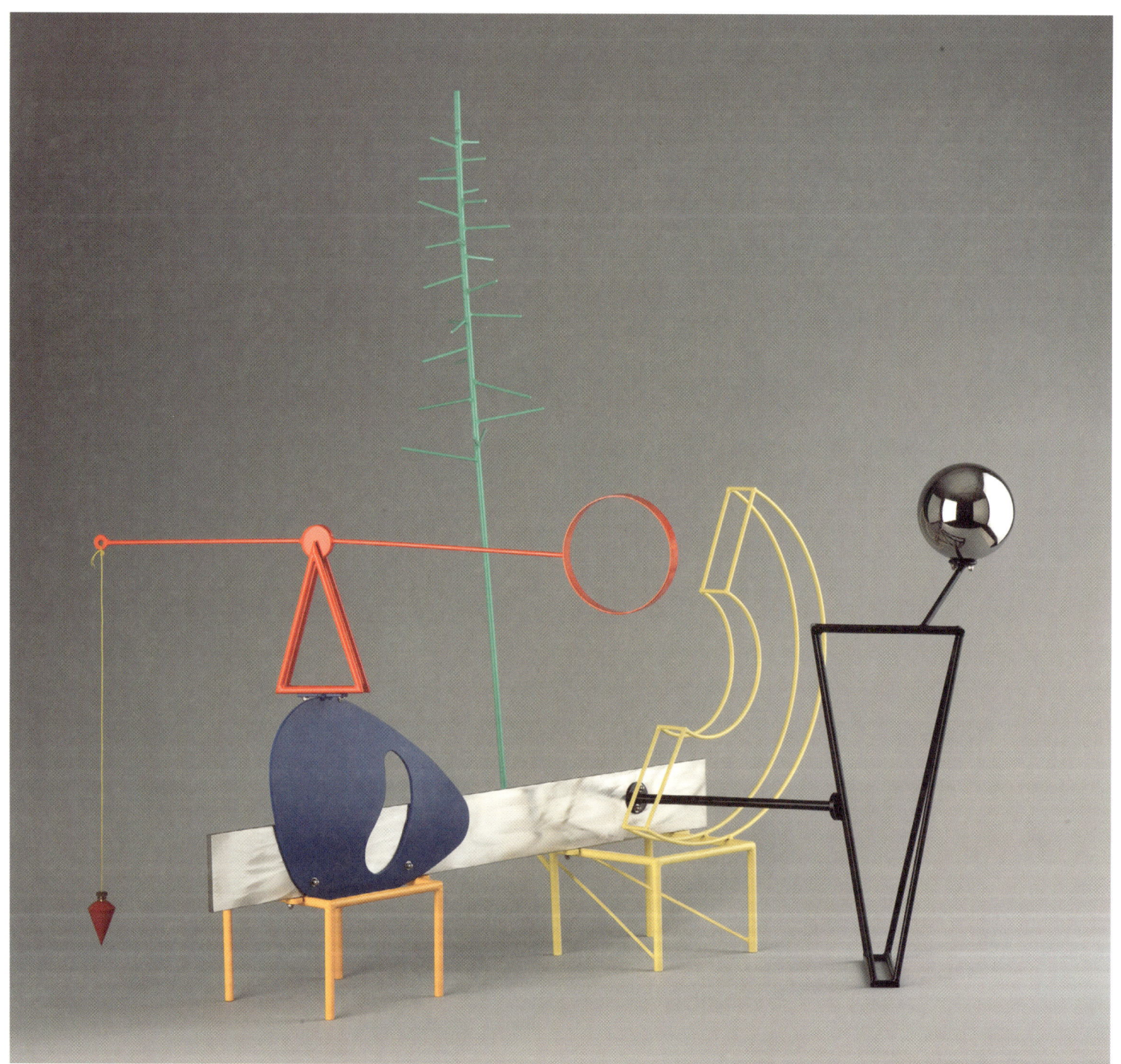

Route 36 Tree, HOKKAIDO, 1993, 32.5" x 24" x 30", Stainless Steel, enamel

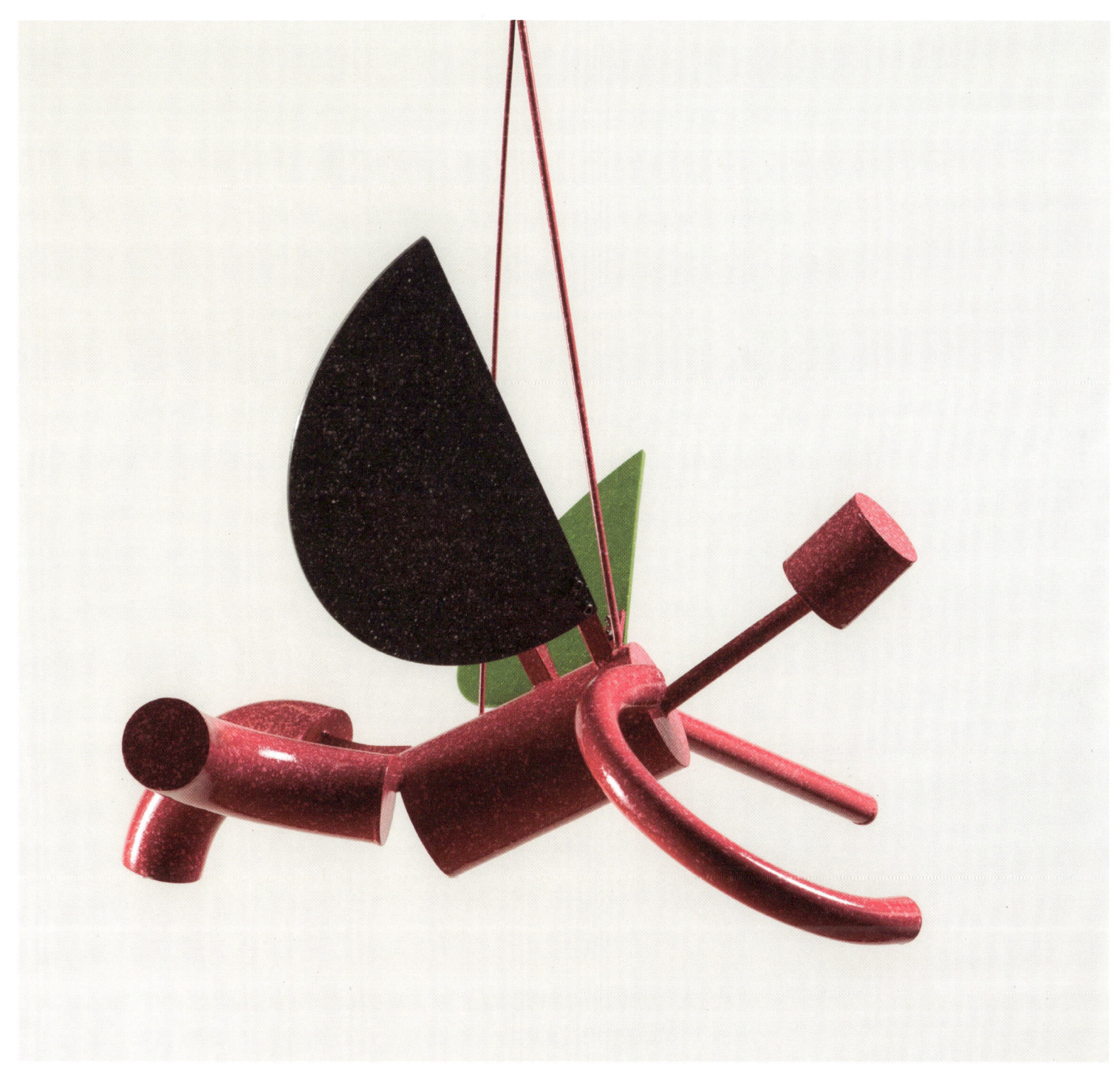

Angel Rosa, Sculpture, 2011, 20" x 21" x 25", Steel, enamel

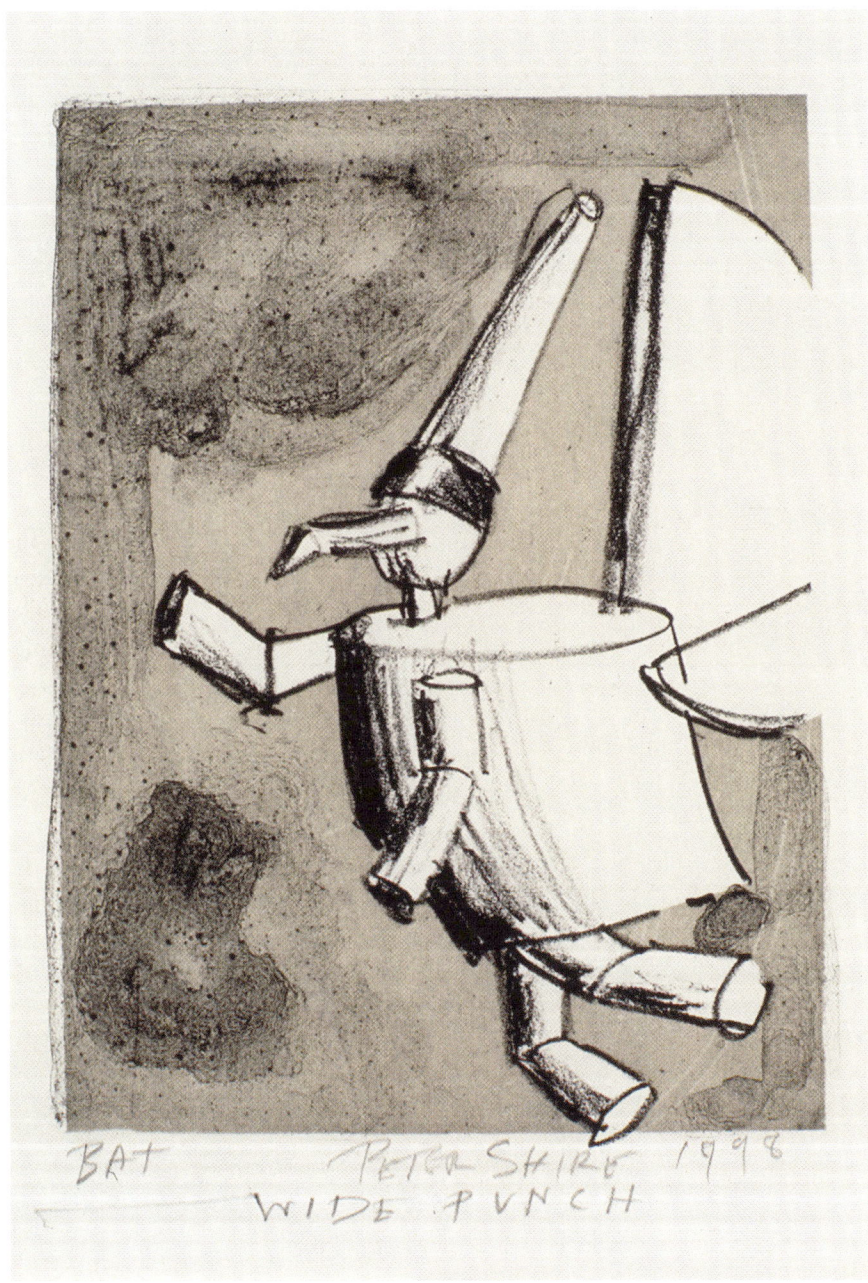

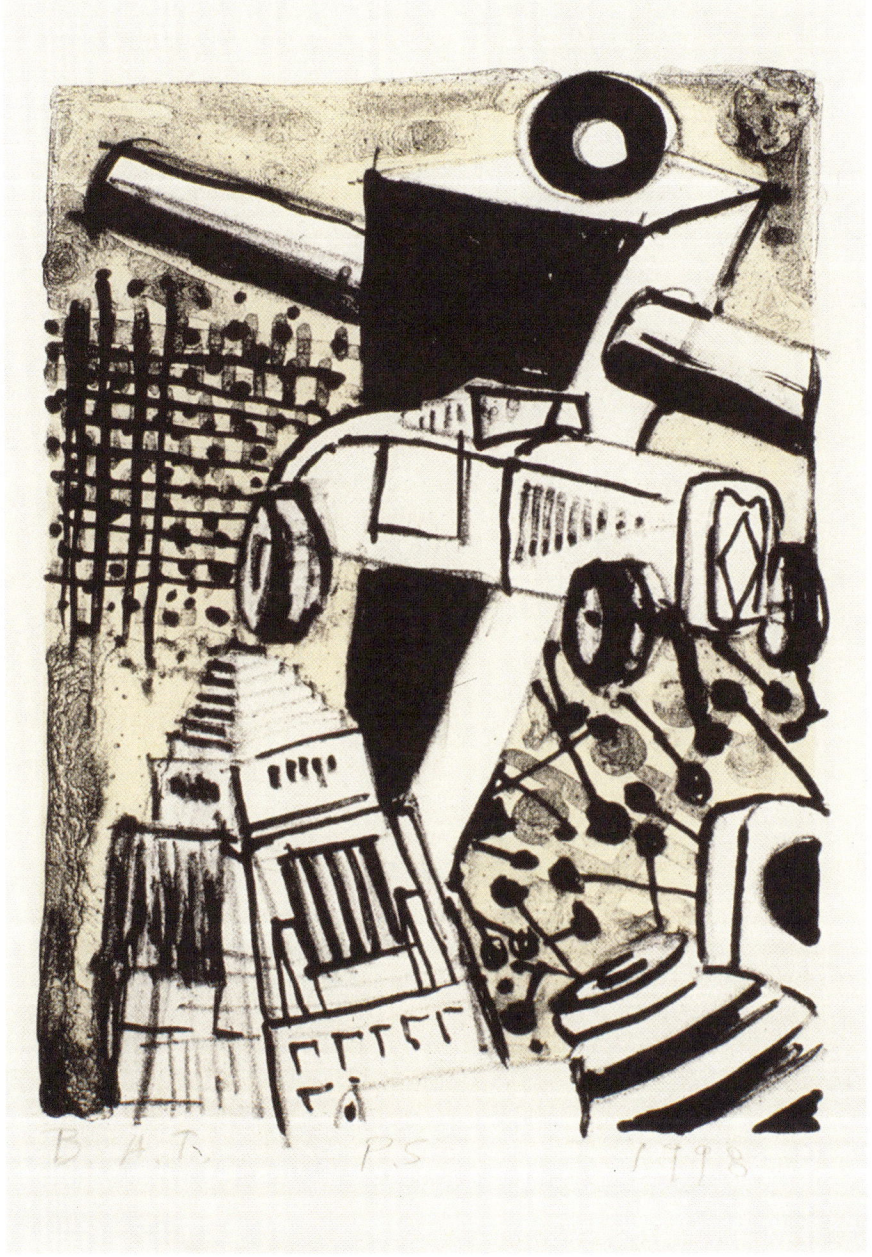

Wide Punch, Print, 1998, 13" x 9 1/2", Lithograph   **Tall,** Print, 1998, 13" x 10", Lithograph

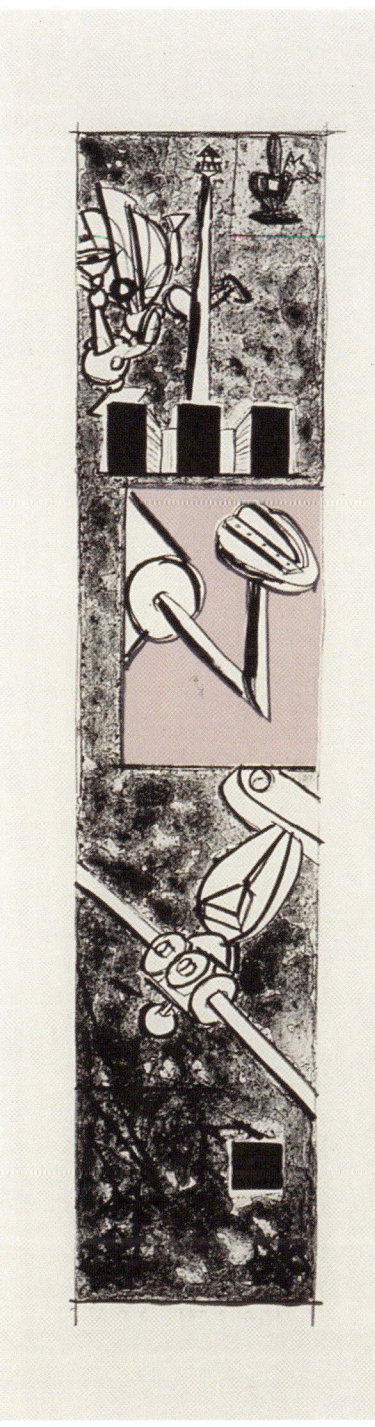

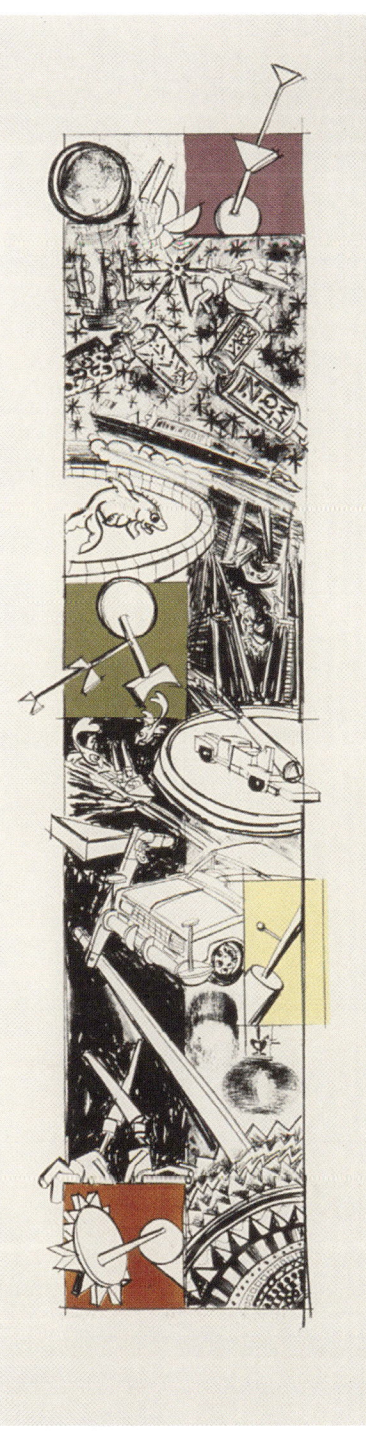

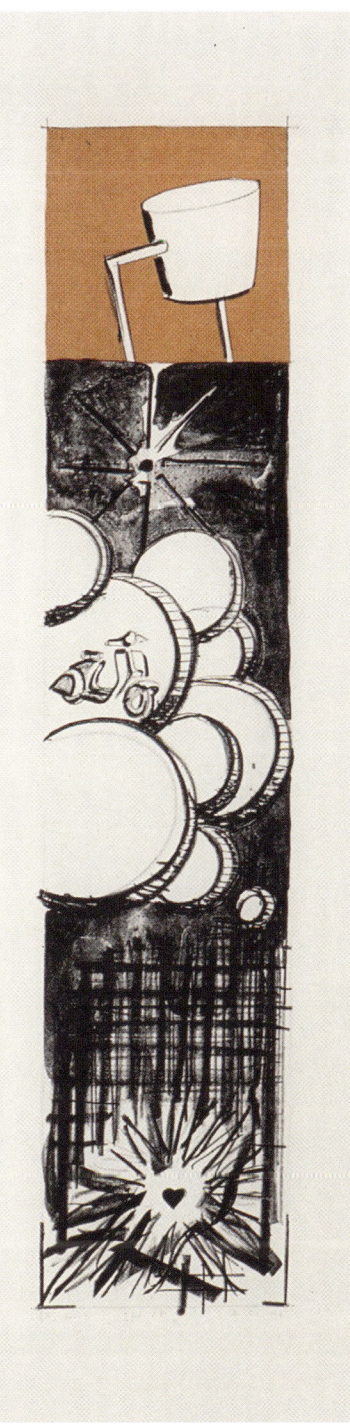

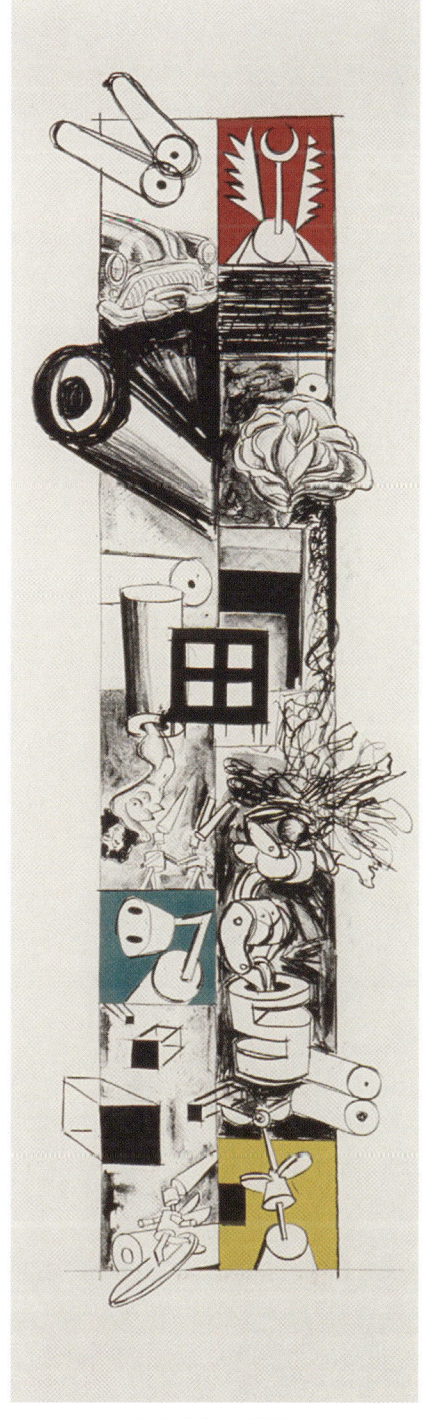

Diva, Print, 1998,
23 1/4" x 8", Lithograph

To Mauro, Print, 1998,
47" x 16", Lithograph

Flex, Print, 1998,
23 1/4" x 8", Lithograph

Lot, Print, 1998,
47" x 17" Lithograph

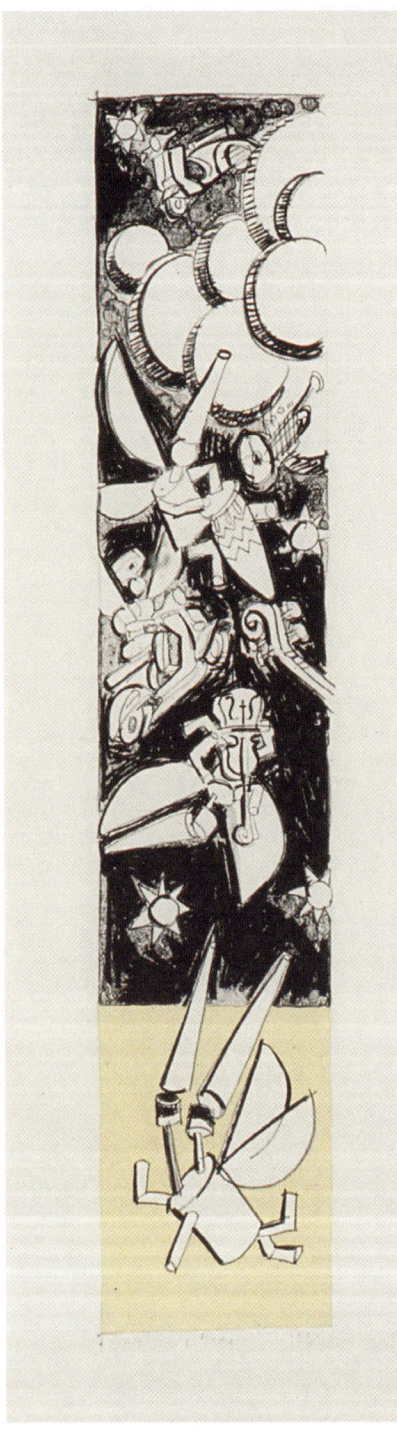

Conga, Print, 1998,
23 1/4" x 8", Lithograph

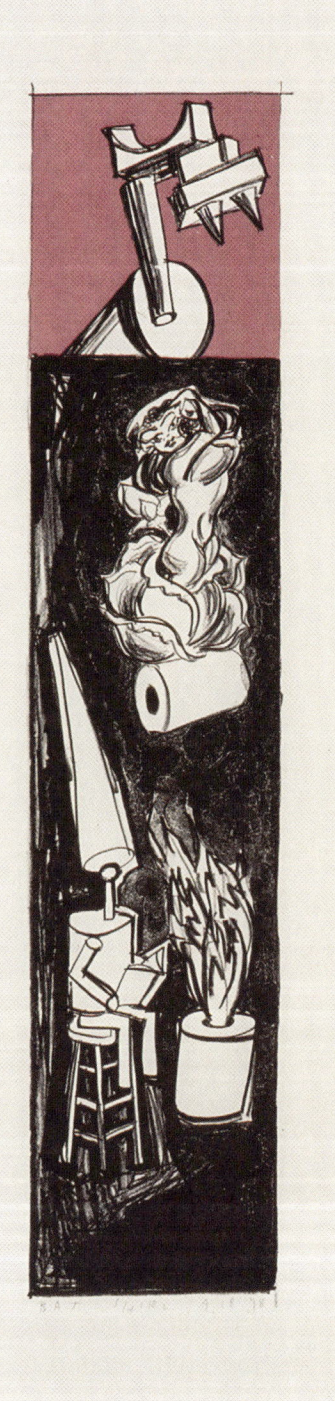

Smoke, Print, 1998,
23 1/4" x 8", Lithograph

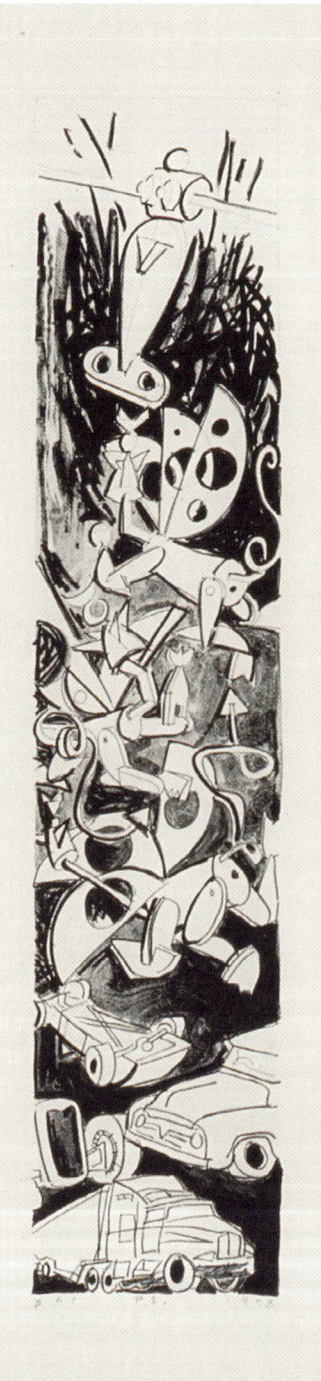

Fooz, Print, 1998,
23 1/4" x 8", Lithograph

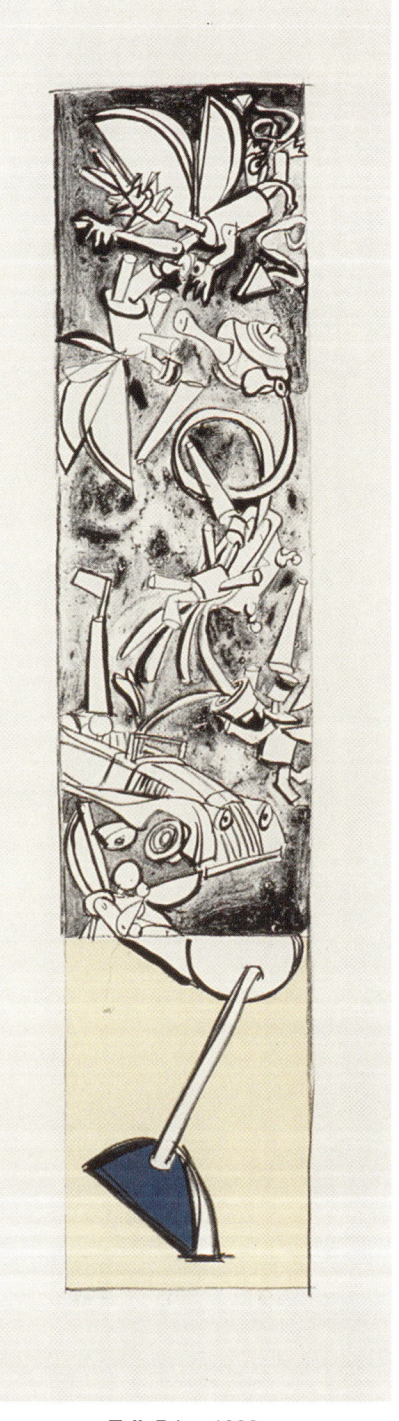

Tail, Print, 1998,
23 1/4" x 8" Lithograph

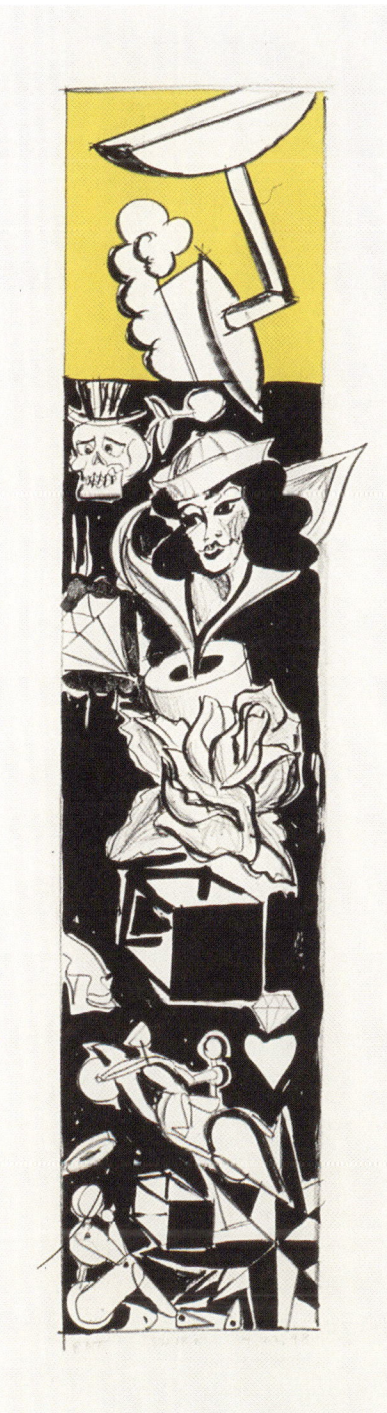

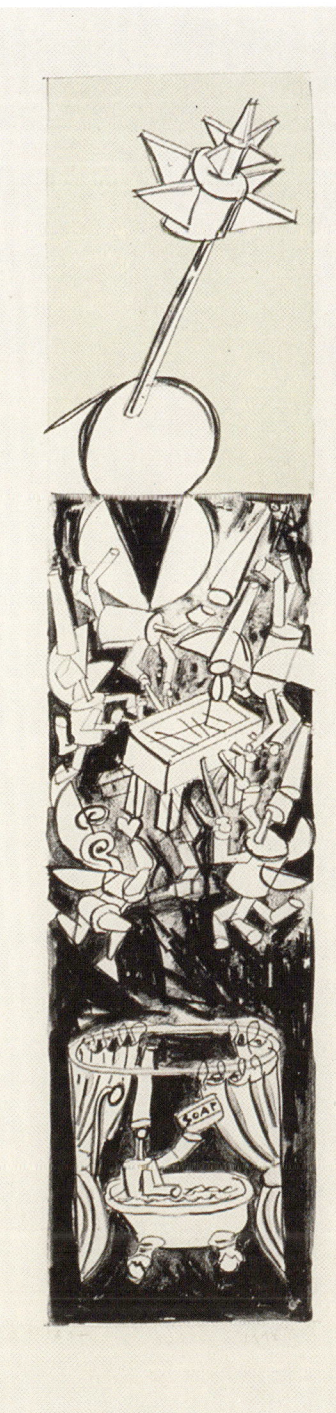

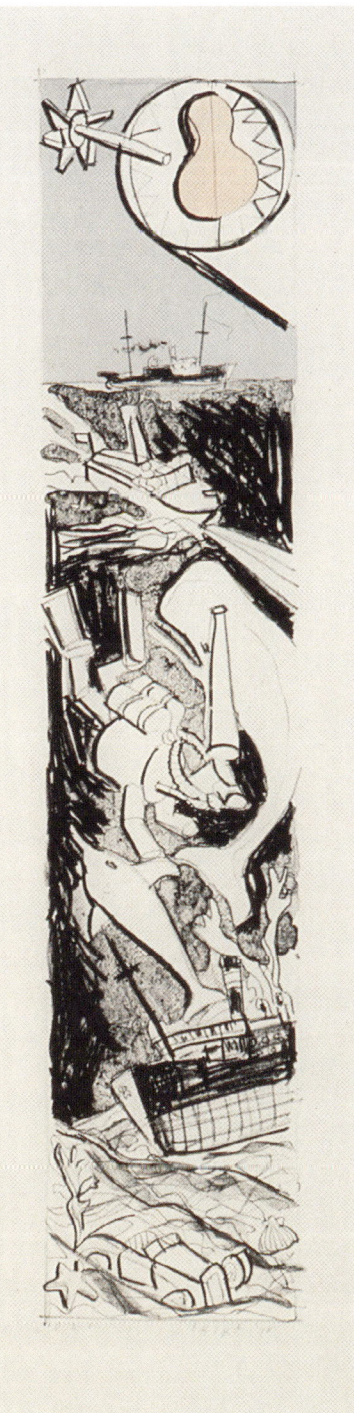

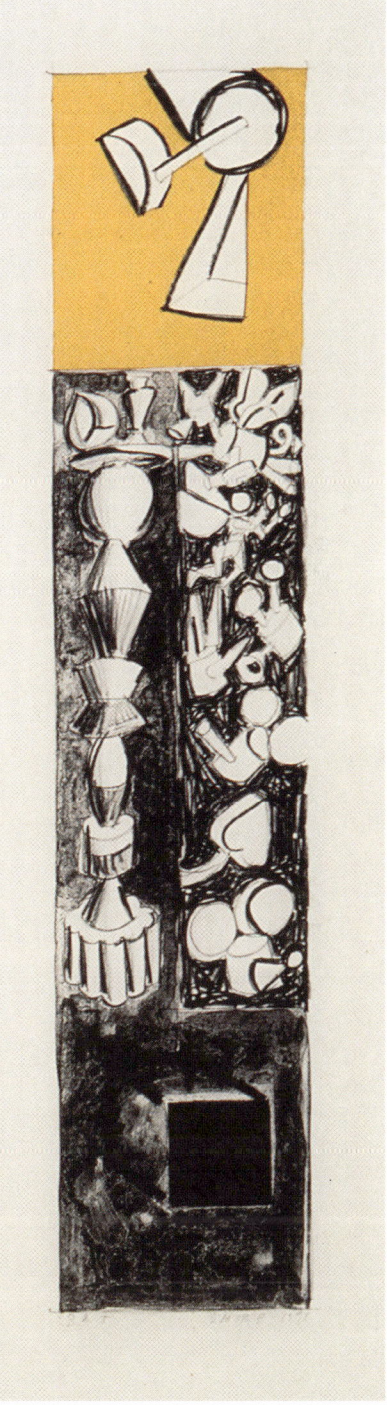

Hey Say, Print, 1998,
23 ¼" x 8", Lithograph

Tub, Print, 1998,
23 1/4" x 8", Lithograph

Deuce, Print, 1998,
23 1/4" x 8", Lithograph

Cube of Space, Print, 1998,
23 1/4" x 8", Lithograph

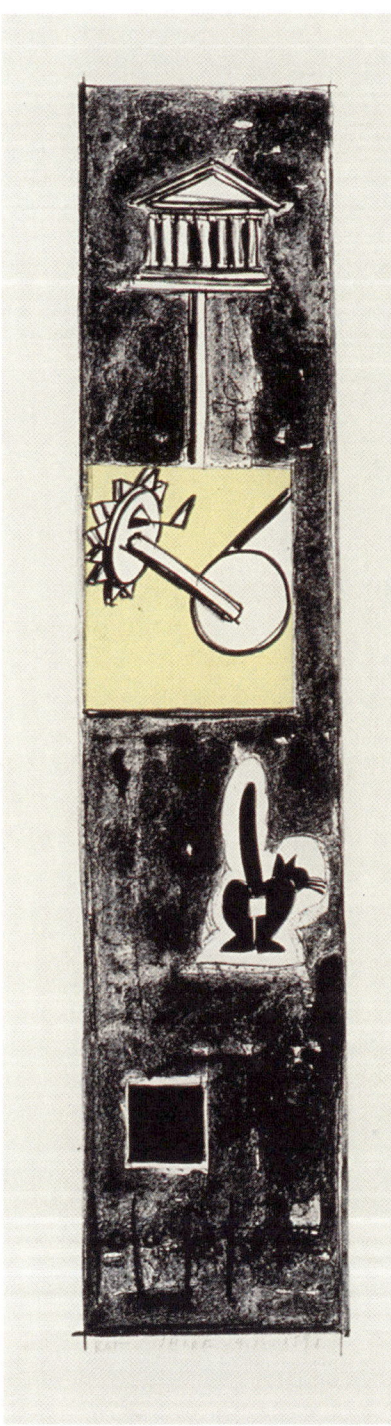

Madelaine, Print, 1998,
23 1/4" x 8", Lithograph

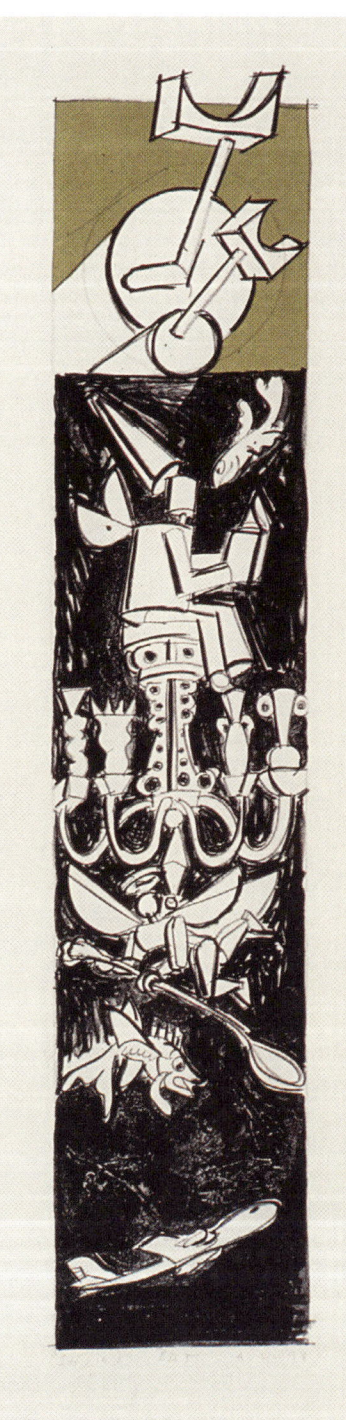

Here I Sit, Print, 1998,
23 1/4" x 8", Lithograph

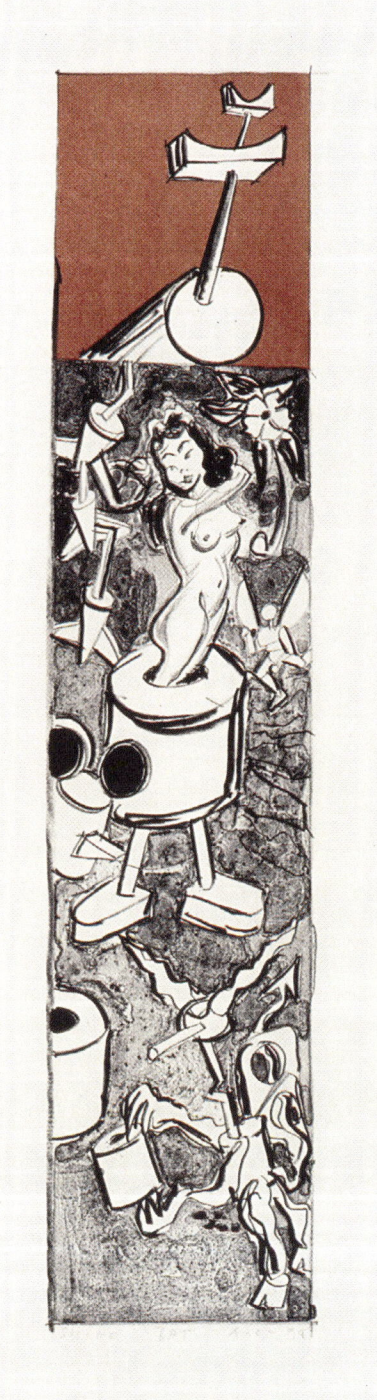

Roll Master, Print, 1998,
23 1/4" x 8", Lithograph

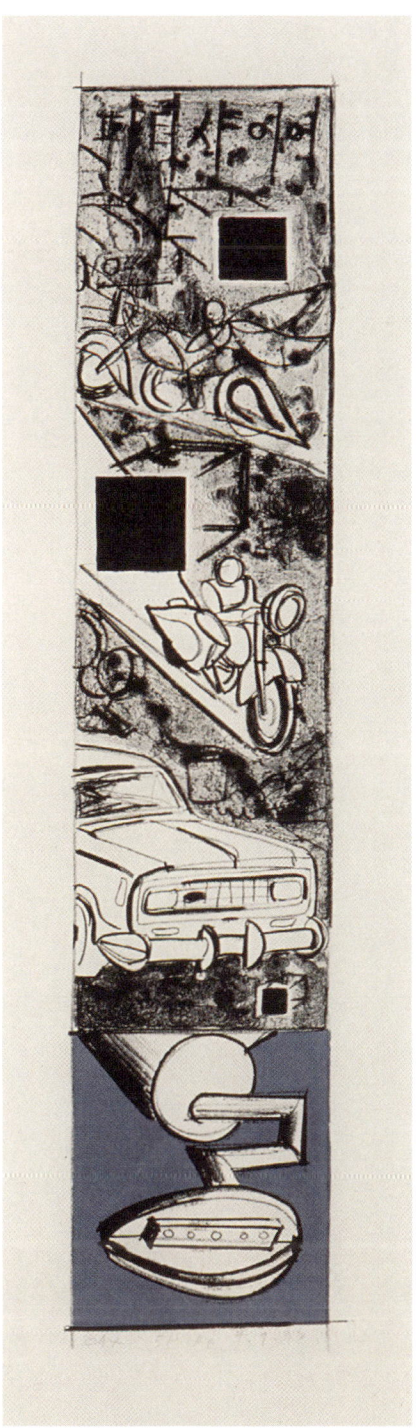

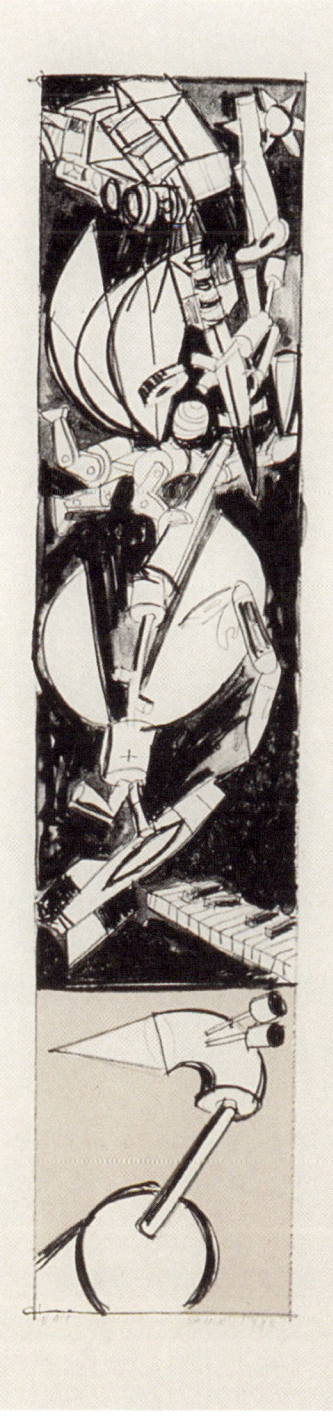

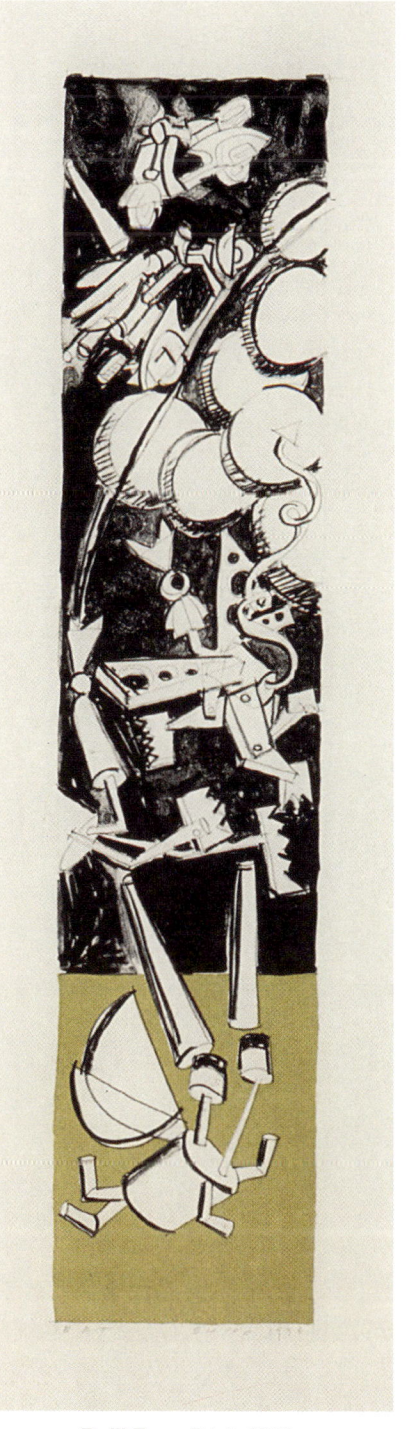

Bumper, Print, 1998,
23 1/4" x 8", Lithograph

Missile Dump, Print, 1998,
23 1/4" x 8", Lithograph

Rolli Free, Print, 1998,
23 1/4" x 8", Lithograph

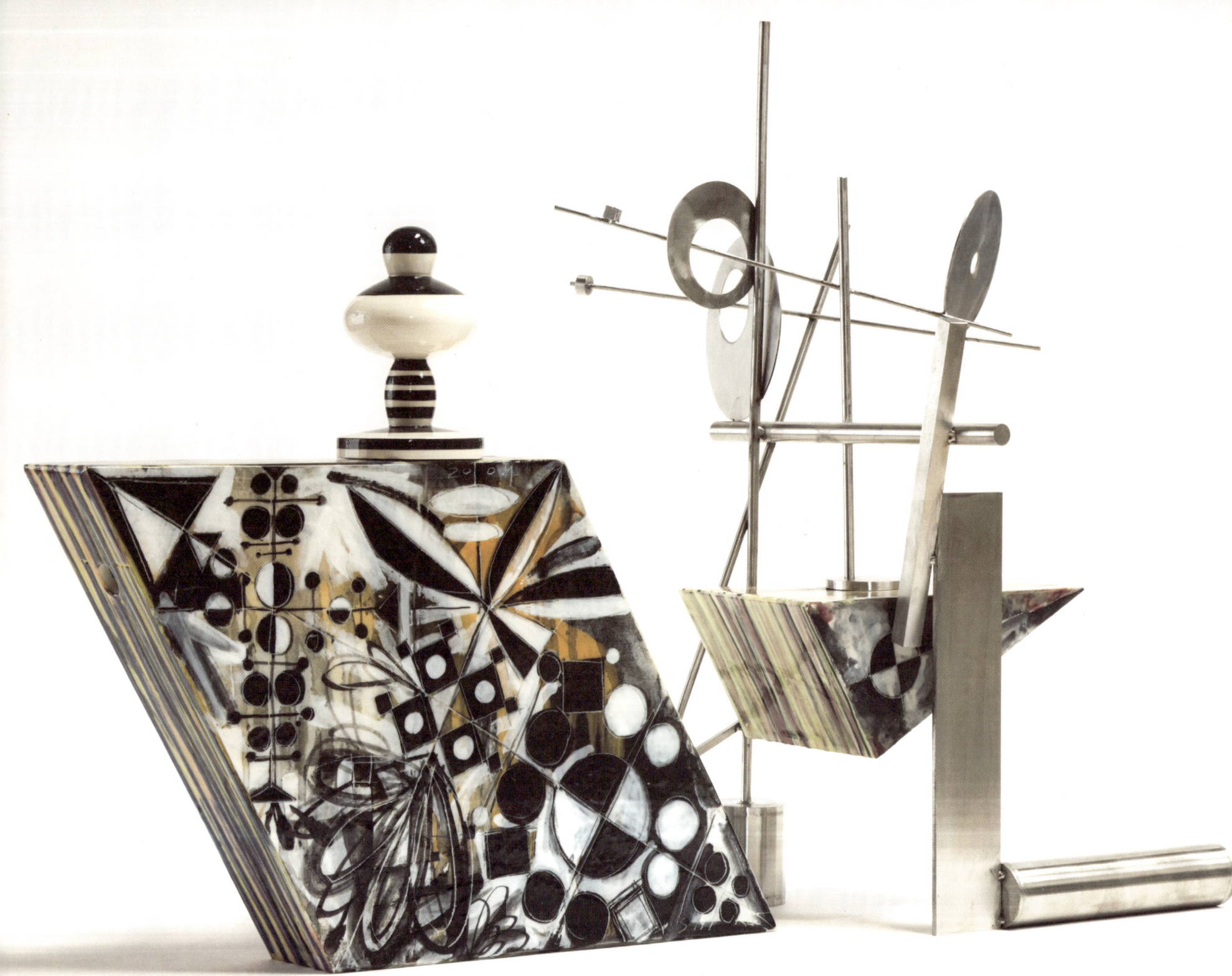

Union Art Gallery

Peter Shire:
A World of Geometrics

Stacko-Lee Series, Teapot, 2006, 21.5" x 32" x 14.5", Ceramic

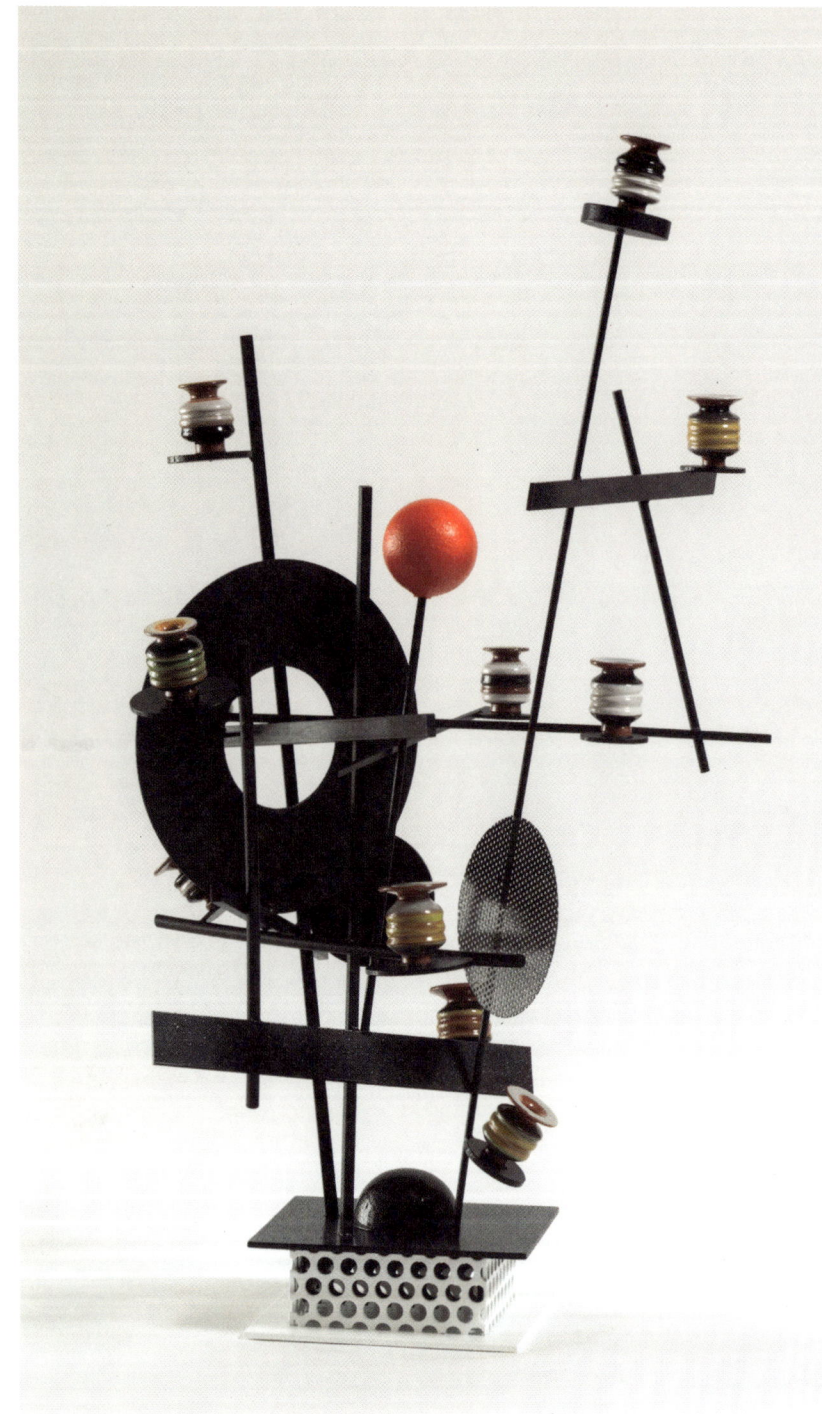

Arboles Locos Negro, 2000, 33" x 18" diameter, Ceramic

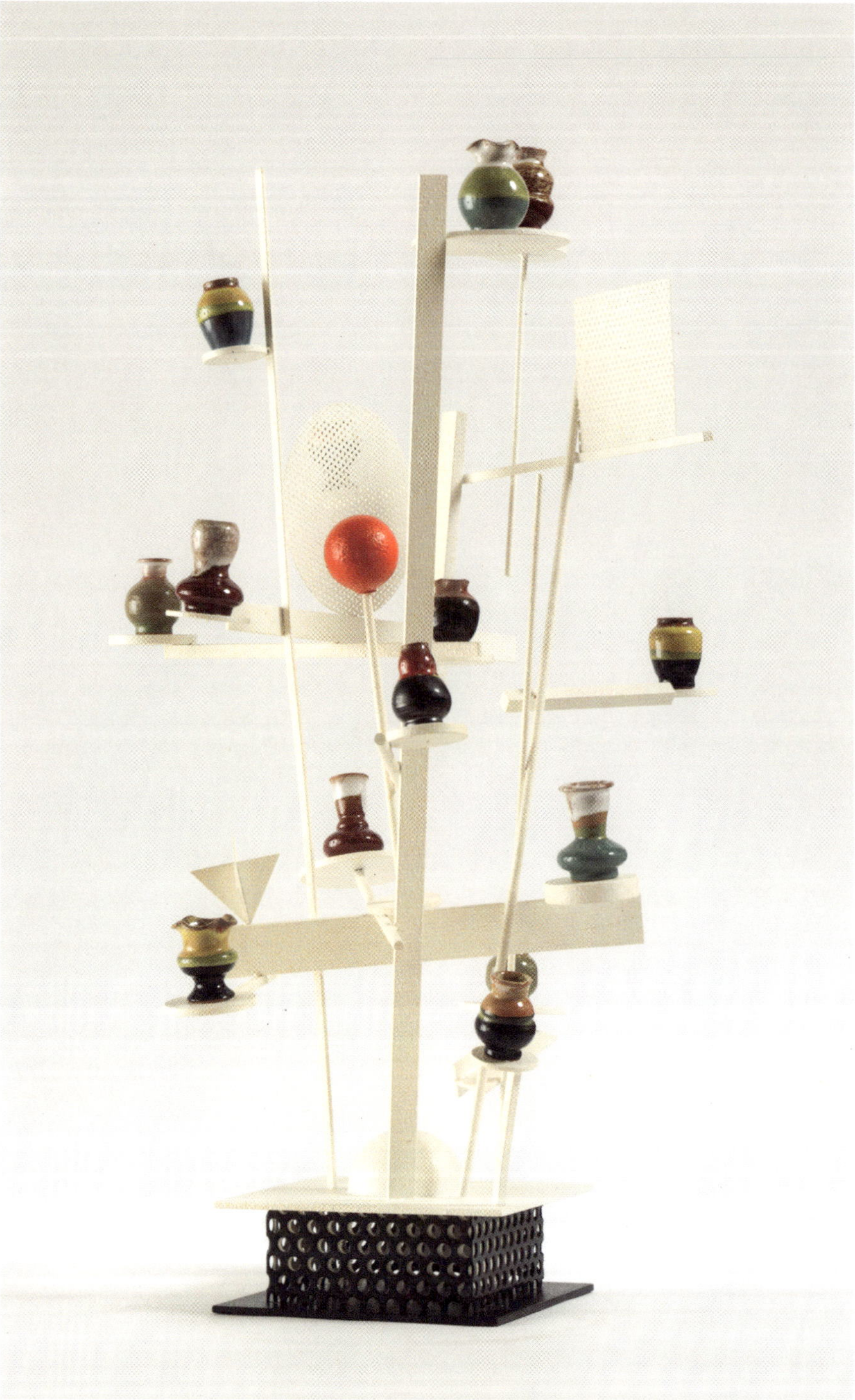

Arboles Locos Blanco, Sculpture, 2000, 32" x 18" diameter, Ceramic

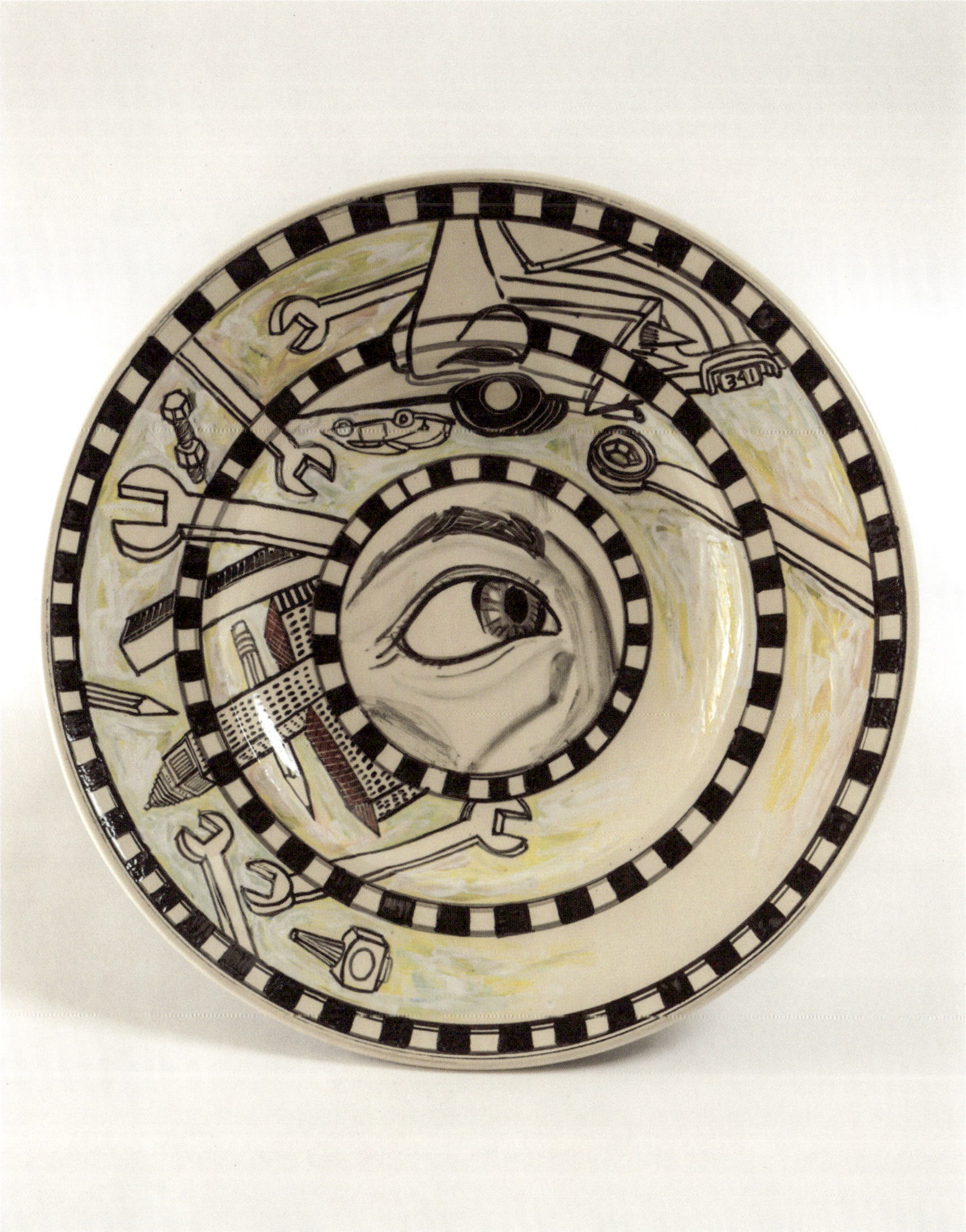

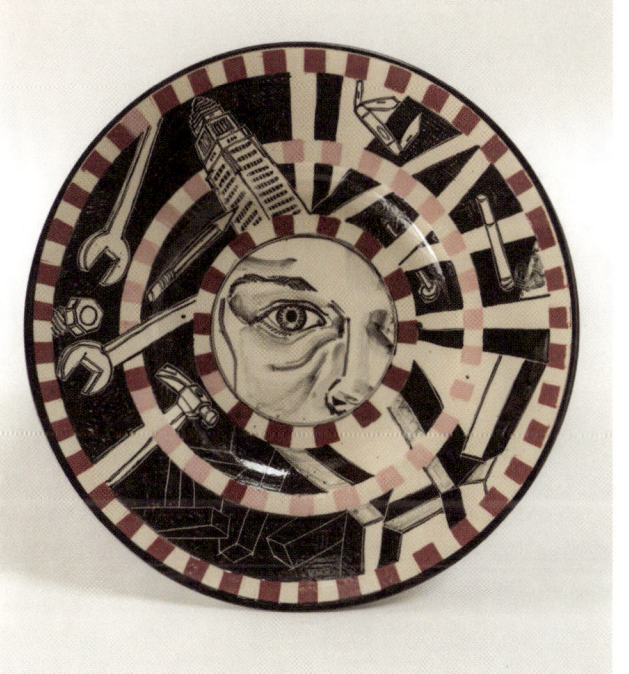

Ava Sees, Platter, 1996, 4" x 19" diameter, Ceramic

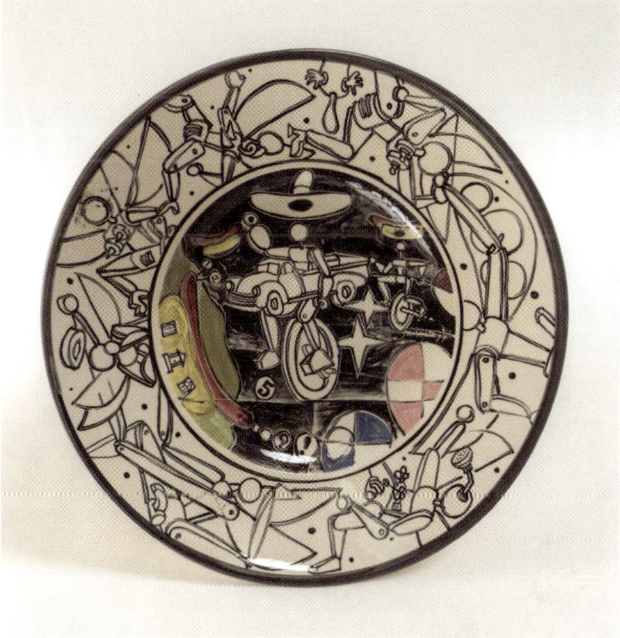

Tinker, Platter, 1996, 4" x 18" diameter, Ceramic

City Life, Platter, 1996, 4" x 18.5" diameter, Ceramic

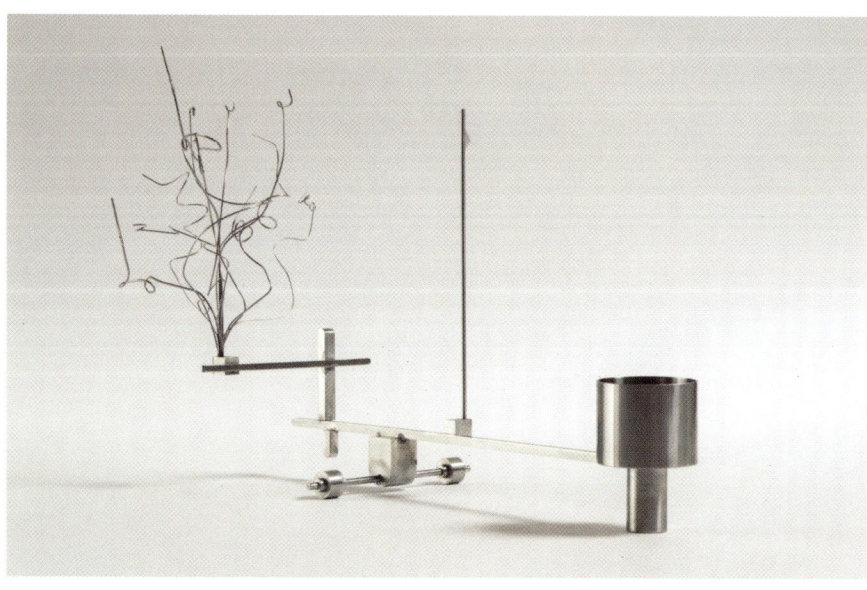

Roller Humo, Cup, 2012, 10.5 x 19 x 9", Stainless Steel

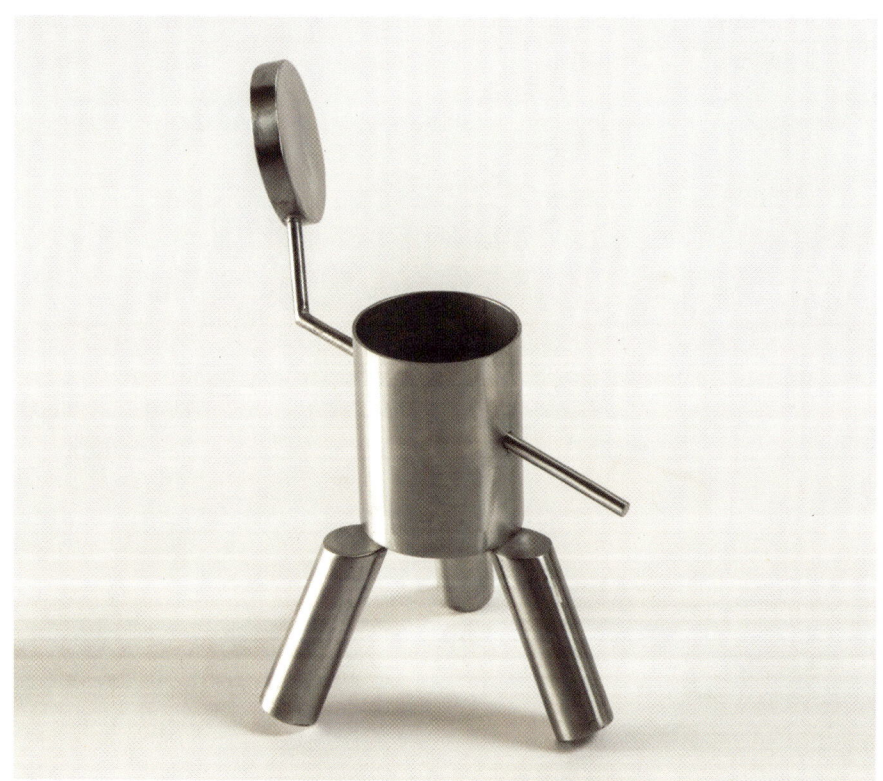

Lolli-Cup, 2012, 8" x 8" x 5", Stainless Steel

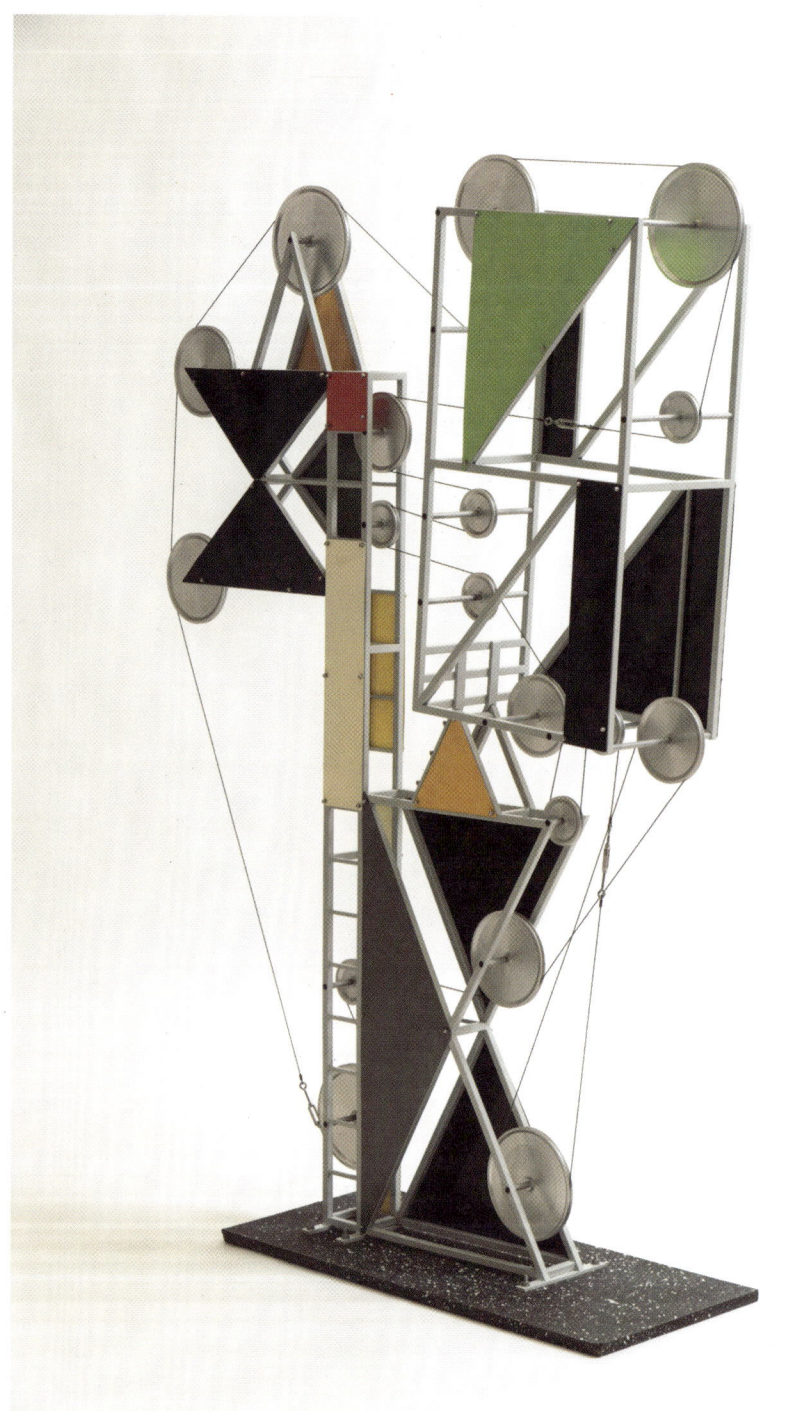

Skyhook, Sculpture Maquette, 1985, Wood, enamel

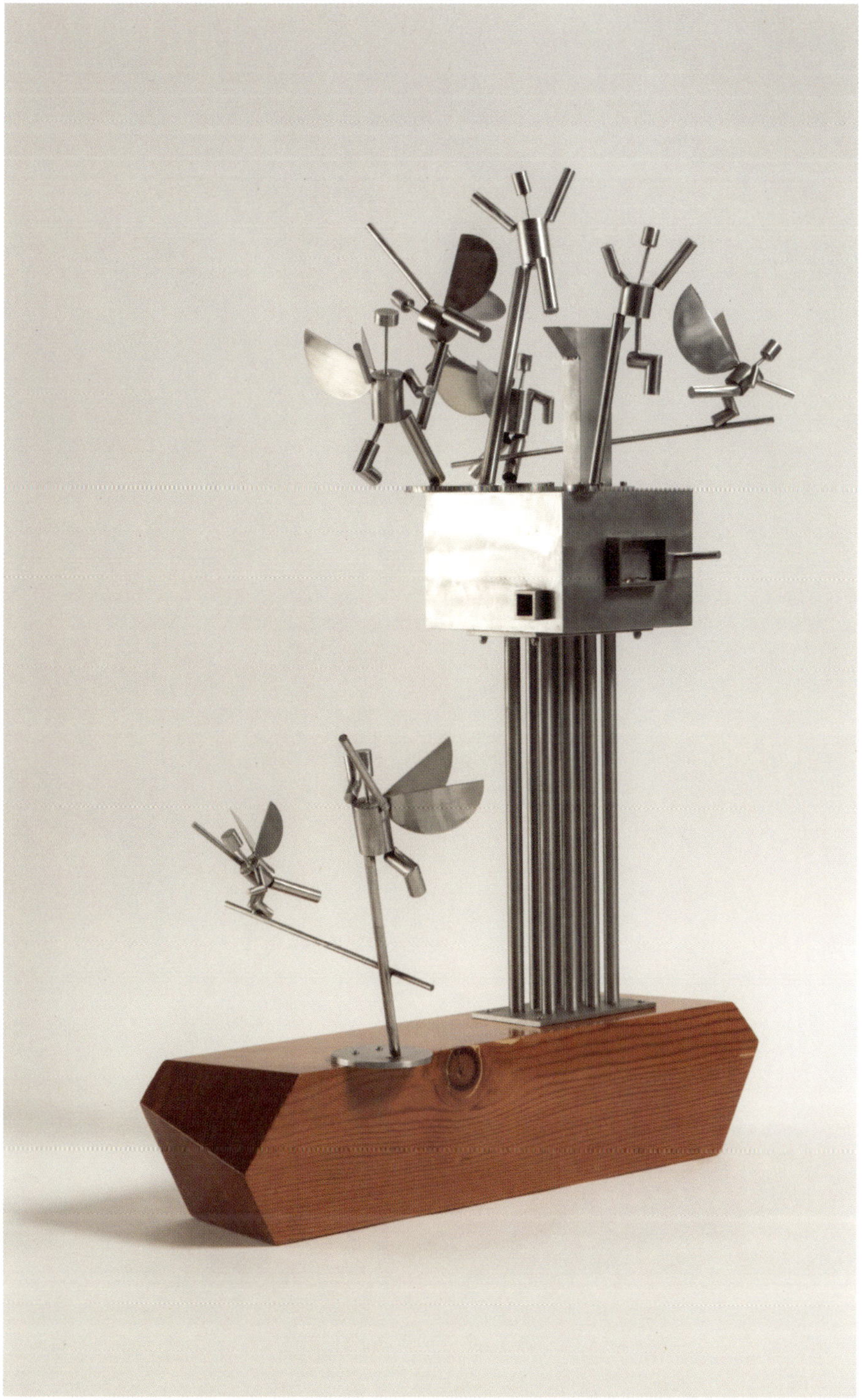

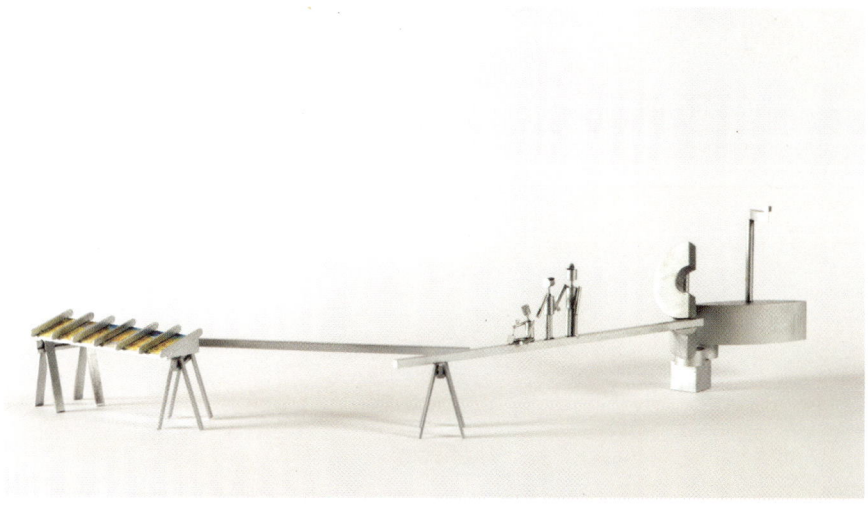

Manhattan, Public Sculpture Maquette, 2010

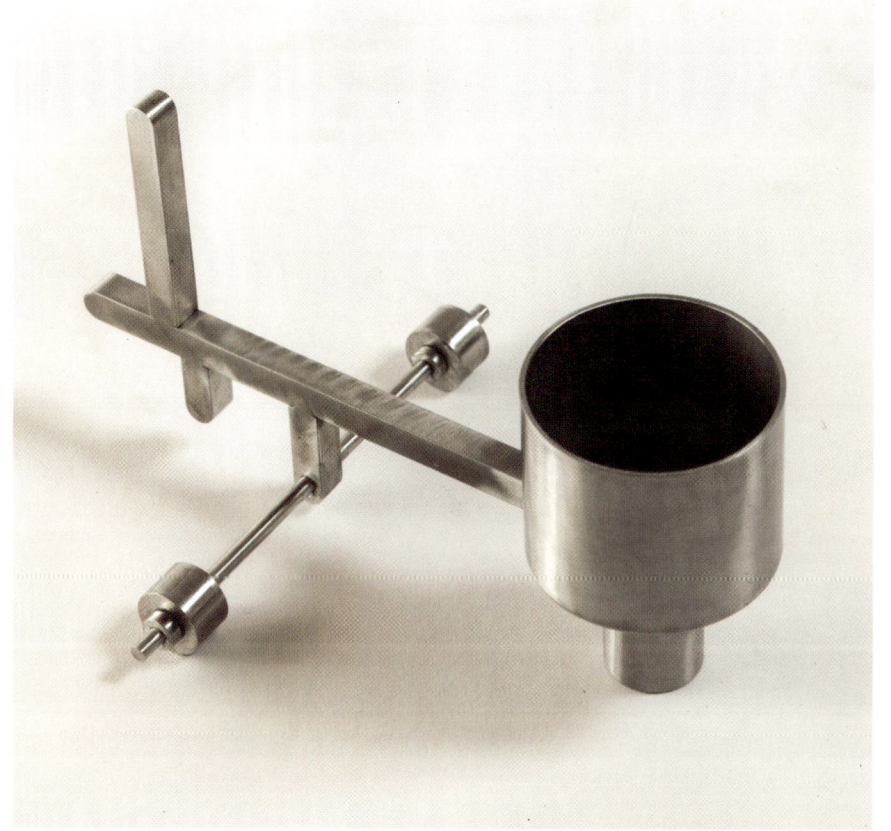

Guardians, Tzedaka Box, 2000, 30" x 26" x 16", Stainless Steel, wood, enamel

Roller One, Cup, 2012, 4.25" x 8.5" x 6.25", Stainless Steel

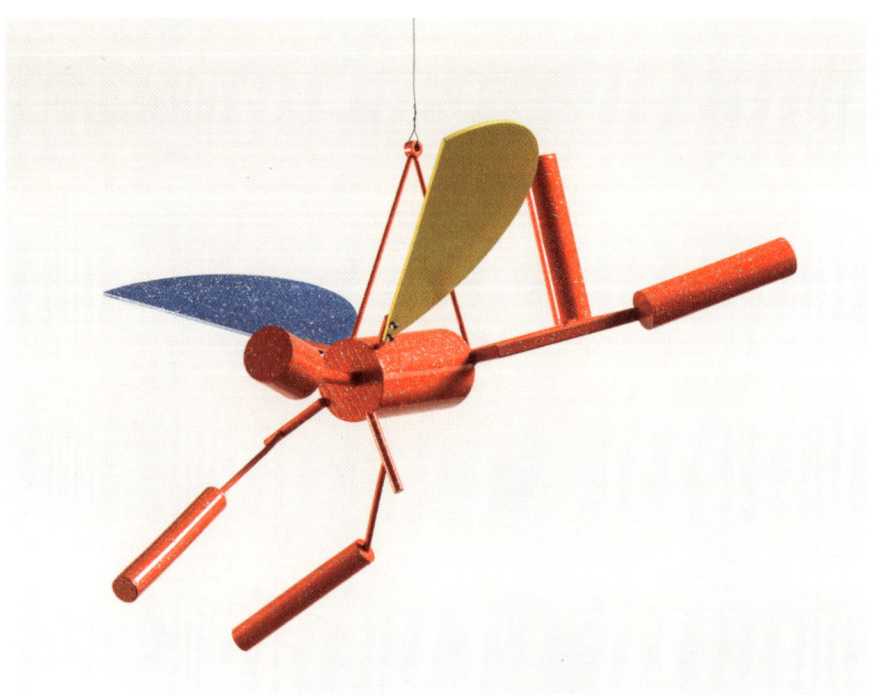

Angel Cremisi, Sculpture, 2011, 12" x 30.5" x 24", Steel, enamel

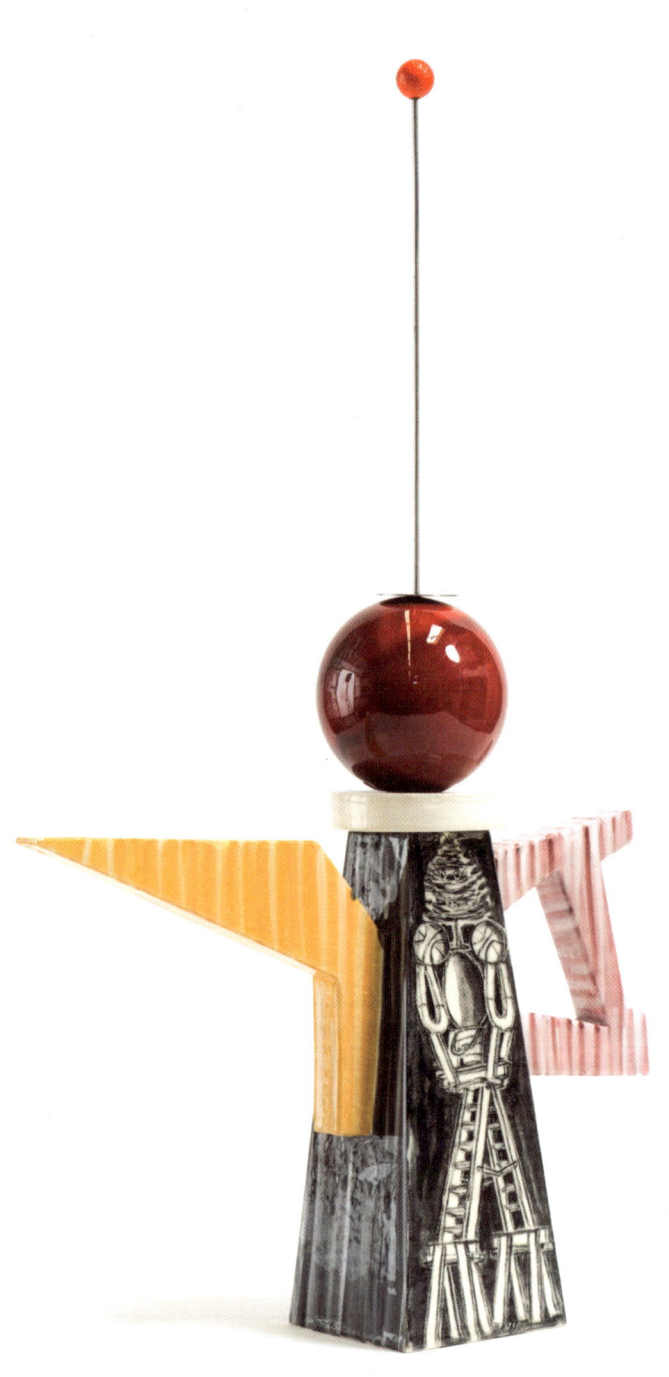

Robo, Milk Carton Teapot, 2010, 26" x 16" x 4", Ceramic

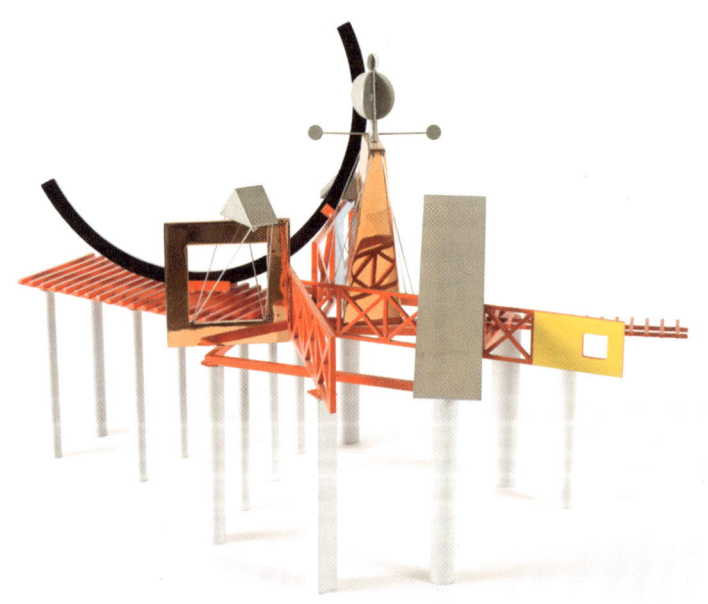

City on the Hill, Public Sculpture Maquette,1997, Steel, enamel

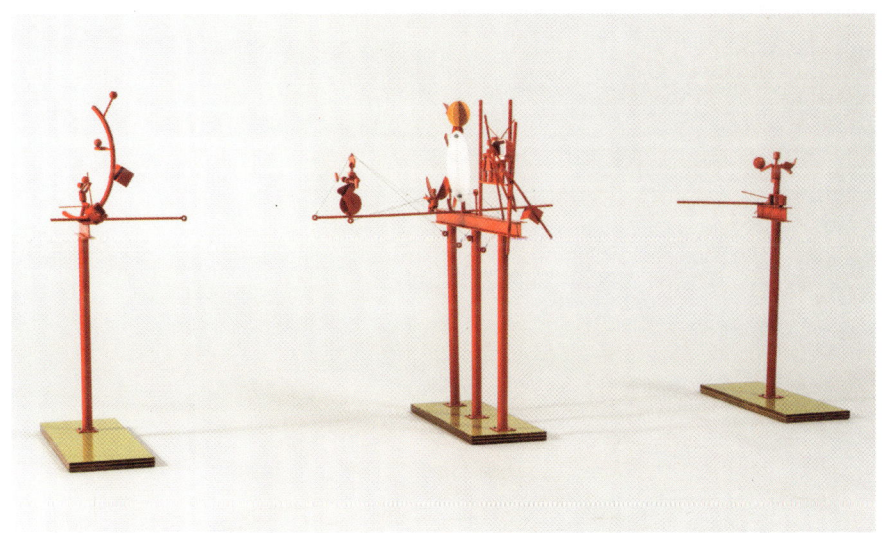

Azusa, Public Sculpture Maquette, 2003, Steel, enamel

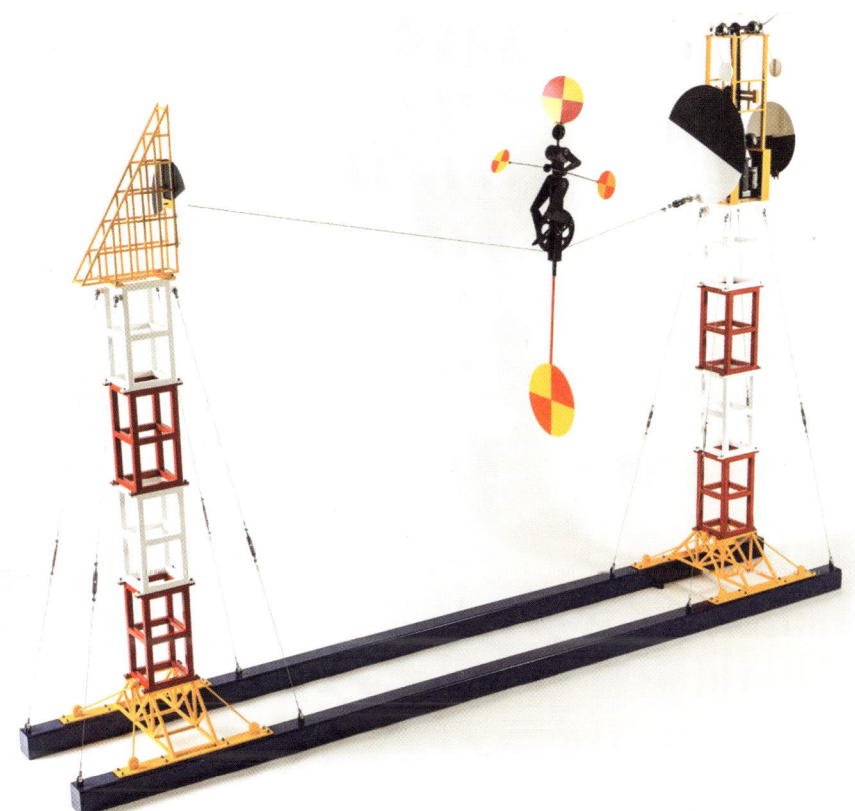

Unicyclist Installation, 1998, (3-parts & unicyclist) 81" x 121" x 20", Steel, enamel

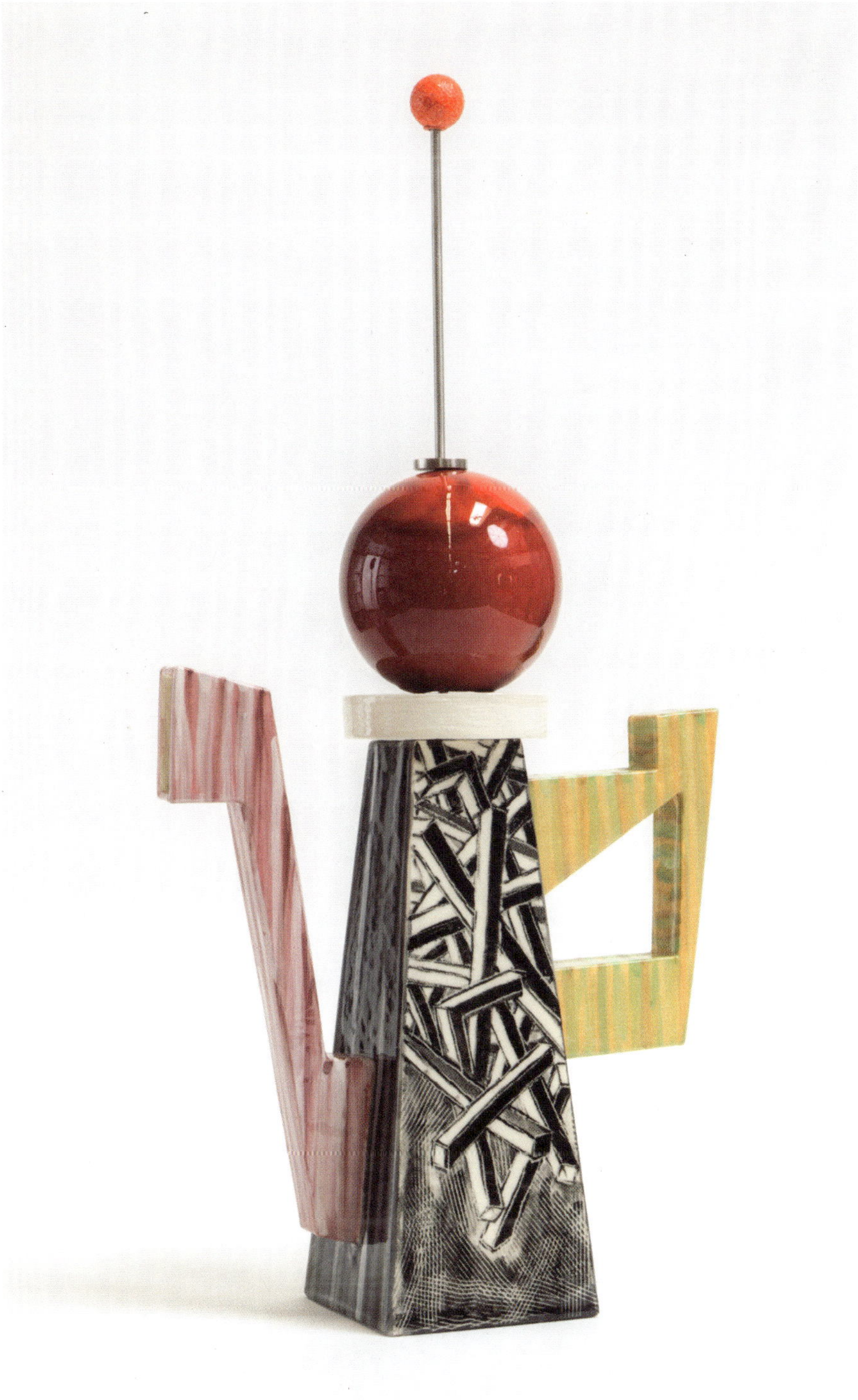

Breathes, Milk Carton Teapot, 2010, 21" x 12" x 4", Ceramic

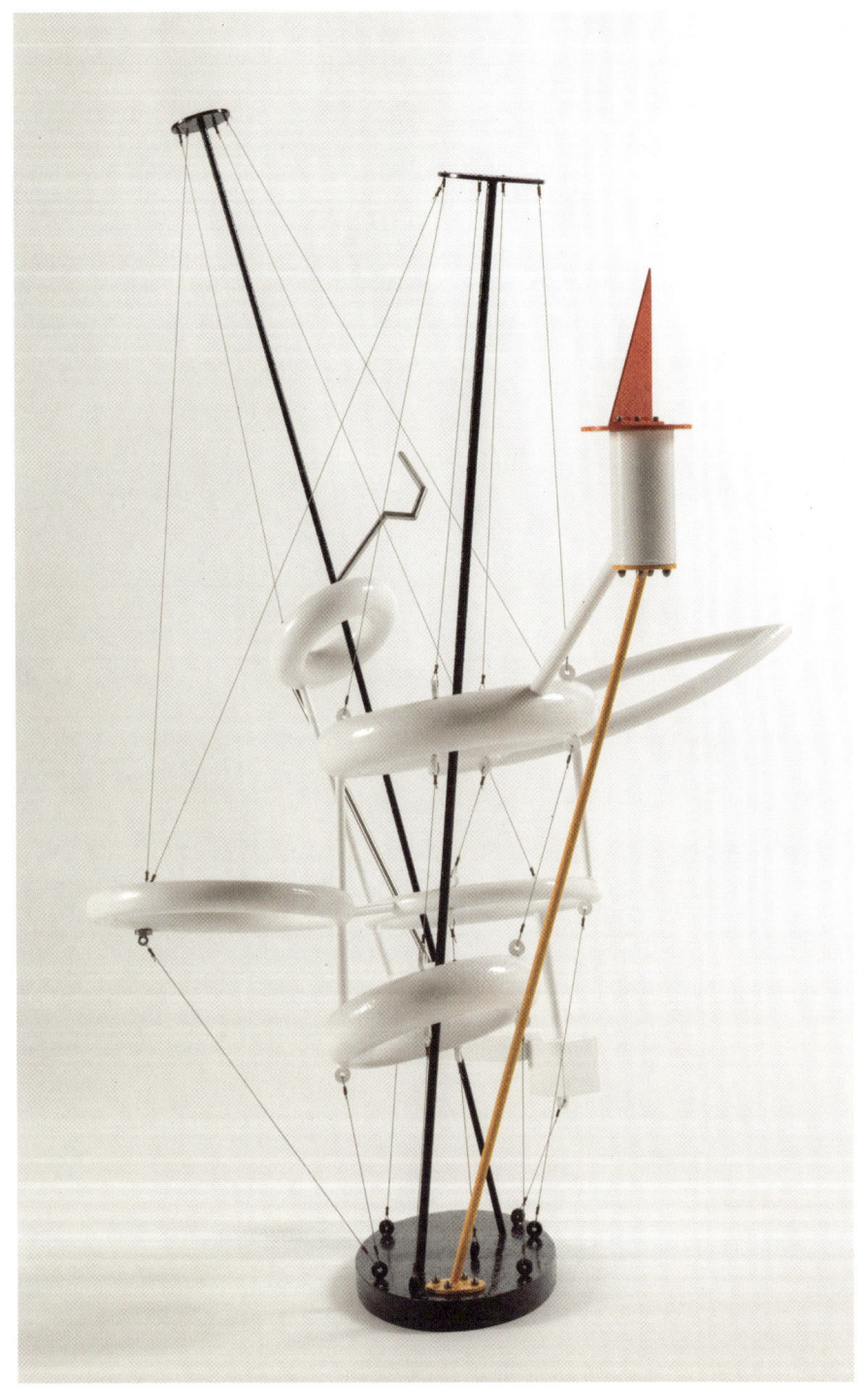

Malevich Station Grande, Teapot, 2006, 48.5" x 37.5" x 27", Steel, chrome, enamel

San Mateo Flag, Cup, 2012, 27.75" x 17" x 15.5", Stainless Steel

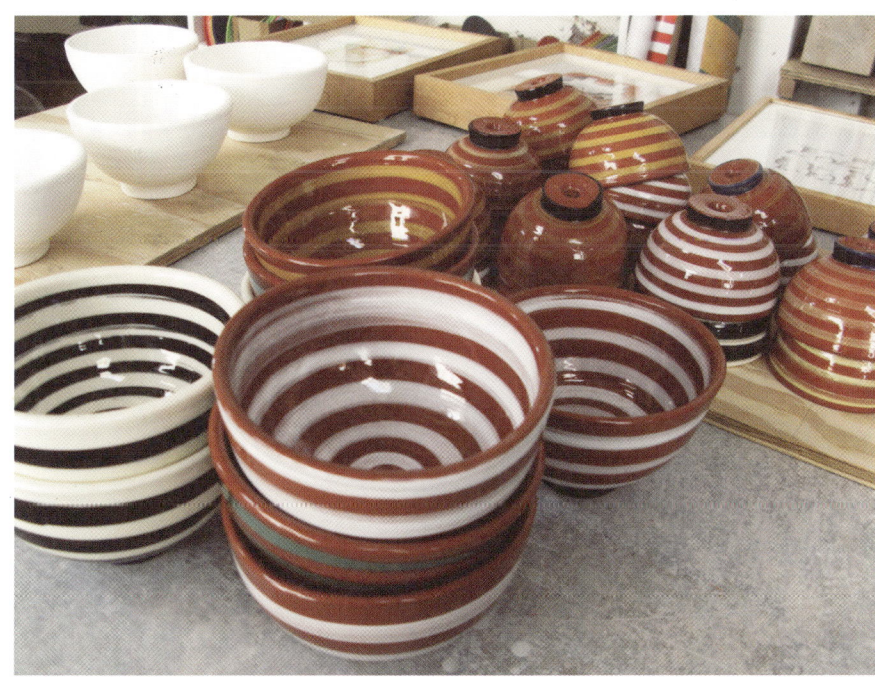

Selection, Echo Park Pottery, 2012, Ceramic

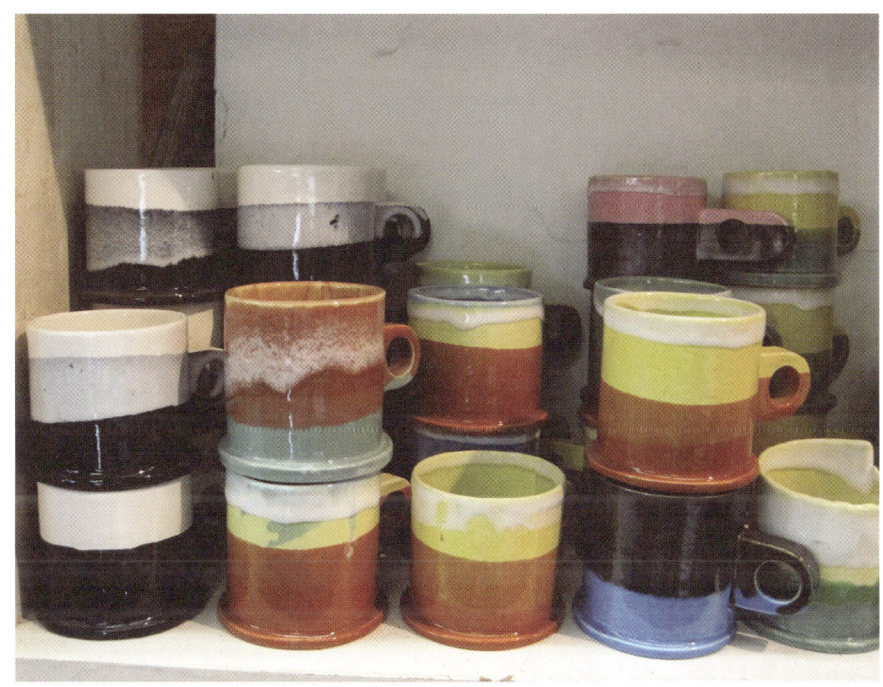

Selection, Echo Park Pottery, 2012, Ceramic

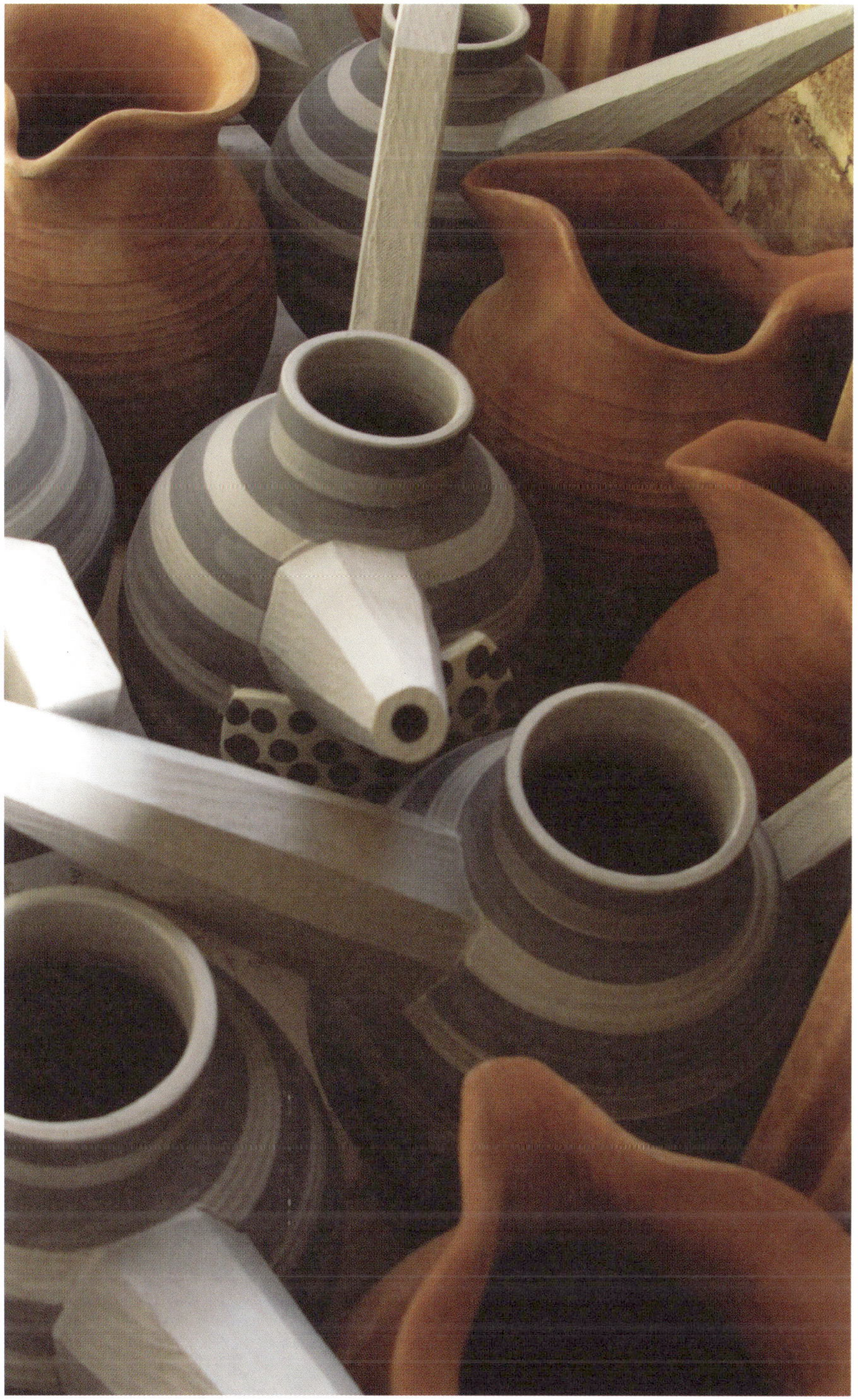

Selection, Echo Park Pottery, 2012, Ceramic

BIOS

Rod Parker

Rod Parker studied typography and bookbinding at the London College of Printing. After a decade of professional practice in identity and branding design he joined the faculty of the School of Art at LSU in 1995, and became Director of the School in 2008. He helped establish the School's Digital Art program, and he is an Associate Professor of Art and a member of the Graduate Faculty.

Jordana Pomeroy

Jordana Pomeroy received her B.A. from Bryn Mawr College and Ph.D. from Columbia University. She has published widely on the subject of collecting and museum building in 19th-century England. Dr. Pomeroy joined the LSU Museum of Art as its executive director in 2012.

Jo Lauria

Jo Lauria is an independent curator and an art and design historian, with a degree in art history from Yale University and in studio art from Otis College of Art and Design. She was decorative arts curator at the Los Angeles County Museum of Art (LACMA), specializing in modern and contemporary decorative arts, craft, and design. She has published extensively, organized numerous exhibitions, and produced and directed multimedia presentations and documentary films.

Darius A. Spieth

A specialist in early modern art, Darius A. Spieth is Associate Professor at Louisiana State University. Besides articles and museum catalogs dealing with art and design history, he has published *Napoleon's Sorcerers: The Sophisians* (University of Delaware Press, 2007). He received his BA from the University of Nebraska-Lincoln, an MA from the University of Illinois at Urbana-Champaign, an MBA from the International University of Japan, and his PhD from the University of Illinois at Urbana-Champaign.